Before I Wake...
Listening to God in Your Dreams

Before I Wake...

Listening to God in Your Dreams

ABRAHAM SCHMITT

Abingdon Press
Nashville

Before I Wake . . .

Listening to God in Your Dreams

Copyright © 1984 by Abingdon Press

Library of Congress Cataloging in Publication Data

SCHMITT, ABRAHAM.
Before I wake—listening to God in your dreams.
1. Dreams—Religious aspects—Christianity.
I. Title.
BF1091.S32   1984   248.4   83-15912

ISBN 0-687-02605-9

Scripture noted TEV is from the Good News Bible, Today's English
Version—Old Testament: Copyright © American Bible Society 1976; New
Testament: Copyright © American Bible Society 1966, 1971, 1976.

MANUFACTURED BY THE PARTHENON PRESS AT
NASHVILLE, TENNESSEE, UNITED STATES OF AMERICA

CONTENTS

FOREWORD

Five teenagers raised their hands. Suddenly they had something to share. The speaker's remarks seemed to give them permission to accept their own experience.

"I had a dream," the speaker had said. And after she had told the dream and explained its meaning the youths had many questions. Is it O.K. to talk about dreams? Can we know the meaning? Won't people think I'm weird if I talk about my dreams?

Young people are not the only ones who ask such questions! Too often we think of our dreams as idle and meaningless. Yet it is well established that nearly everyone dreams four to seven times every night. We also know that many people do not remember their dreams. So the question continues: Should I pay attention to my dreams?

You have just picked up a book that not only will help you discover the meaning of your dreams, but will open a new gateway to the life of the soul and a way to listen to God.

Dreams are so common, yet so poorly understood. Here are several well-known examples of dreams which guided personal destinies.

Think of the familiar song "We Are Climbing Jacob's Ladder." Jacob took his dream seriously. God had a message for him. When Jacob awoke he thought, "The Lord is here! He is in this place, and I didn't know it!" (Gen. 28:16 TEV).

Paul began a missionary journey. He and his travel companions were unclear as to where they should focus their ministry. Finally, Paul received direction from a vision in which a man from Macedonia begged them to come to that land (Acts 16:9).

The captain of a slave ship had a dream. In the dream Christ met him and, through highly symbolic language, called him to repent of his sinful life. He was deeply moved and amazed by Christ's salvation. From that captain's pen we have the well-loved hymn "Amazing Grace."

Our own dreams, the Bible, and church history provide us with hundreds of examples. Dreams have been a concern of prominent Christian writers for twenty centuries. And in the past hundred years, social scientists and scholars have turned their attention toward dreams in a new way.

Now Abraham Schmitt has given us a book to fill that vacant spot on the Christian life bookshelf. When I had finished reading it, I understood why he calls dreams the language of the soul. I could identify with his experiences and with those of his clients. Some of my own vivid dreams came back to me from far out of the past. And as I followed the ten steps to dream understanding, I began to remember my present dreams. I was dreaming more than I had thought. By following the dream in chapter 3 and its analysis, I gained new insight into the understanding of my dreams.

Abraham Schmitt has pulled back the curtain of the inner chambers of his soul to reveal a little of his inner life. He does this with courage and discretion. The real value, though, is that I now have the courage to look within myself with new understanding. As I read the various chapters, I was led to focus on my own inner life, my dreams, and the needs of my own soul. Dr. Schmitt shows reverence and sensitivity for the mysteries of the soul, and through his insights and honest sharing we are led to understanding of ourselves and reverence for the God who created us in his image.

The style of the book is straightforward and sometimes as gripping as a novel. The reader not only will discover new personal insights but learn to share them with other Christians as a means of inspiration, nurture, and mutual support.

Here is a brilliant and sensible guide to listening to God through our dreams. The methods, the explanations, and the language are succinct and easily understood. All of us, with reasonable effort, can profit from this imaginative aid to a richer faith through a better understanding of our dreams.

Laban Peachey, Ed.D., in
Counseling Psychology

ACKNOWLEDGMENT

I wish to recognize and thank several persons who were of special help to me as I wrote this book.

My wife, Dorothy, deserves a special thanks for taking my handwritten scrawl and organizing it into sentences, paragraphs, and chapters, and for retyping until it reached its present form.

My children took a unique interest in this book. They quickly caught on to my theory and then freely shared their dreams. At times they arrived at an accurate understanding. On other occasions they asked for help in gaining greater insight. The interpreting of dreams has become a family event.

A group of friends conversed with me on the subject of dreams and their correlation with Scripture: Robert and Lucy Gotwals, Clyde and Jane Landes, Herbert and Marian Wenger, John A. Hostetler, John Bettler, Wilson and Betty Touhsaent.

I also acknowledge the many clients and friends who shared their dreams and granted permission to use them in this book. I am grateful, too, for their assistance in disguising the identifying data to assure anonymity.

PREFACE

When I told my son I was writing a book on dreams, he responded in his typical intuitive and analytical manner. "Oh, I see, Dad. You want to write a book on dreams because you want to be asked to Pharaoh's court and then, like Joseph of the Old Testament, be the interpreter of dreams for the king."

"Well, son," I responded, "you may be partially right, but it would take me a long time to explain my reasons. You may just have to read the book to find the answer."

There is no question that in dealing with dreams we are grappling with the very deep, unconscious level of our beings. It is also a known fact that this deep level is the source of much of our behavior. The more one can get in touch with this level of the self, the more it is possible to be responsible for what one feels, thinks, and does. Dreams provide an avenue to that inner self.

My son's comment startled me, since as a child I was nicknamed Joseph by my siblings because they designated me as my father's favorite. I wonder—is that fact still lingering in my hidden self, so that now I, like Joseph, have become fascinated with dreams?

Dreams have a way of bringing many disjointed parts of the self into a single simple perspective in a way that cannot be done in the waking state, using our conscious rational process. Because of this potentially powerful effect, I wish to ask you, my readers, to invite God to be part of the entire dream-work experience. I believe we are acutely sensitive to very important insights of the self while working with dreams. If God is also present, he can speak to us through these insights, and we can receive direction for living.

Emil Brunner of the University of Zurich implied this when he said, "You are also answerable to God for your dreams," referring to dreams experienced while asleep. When I shared the content of this book with a former student of his, J. C. Wenger, he recalled Dr. Brunner's statement, and then added, "I never understood what my beloved professor meant by that statement. I always assumed that dreams were the product of my mind at play, and thus meaningless. But after listening to your explanation about how to make use of dreams, I now know he meant that dreams are messages from God, and obviously we are accountable for their meaning."

At some deep hidden level, this book has been in the process of evolving for twenty years. During that time I have had very lucid dreams. When I awoke, I understood their meanings as clearly as if I had been spoken to. Because they were so obviously tied to my immediate life experience, I did not doubt that the dreams were conveying a message. Actually, I was unaware that most people do not experience and use dreams in the same way. I sensed God's presence in a dream, and I then responded with a certainty that I was doing God's will. I simply saw no other way to deal with dreams.

Professionally, I knew that the more insight I gained into myself, the more effective I would be in helping others. Since my academic studies and teaching were in the field of personality theory and psychotherapy, I realize that this must have contributed to my search to understand dreams.

Later, as I shared my belief in dreams, I quickly discovered a very receptive audience. Many were certain that specific dreams had spoken to them in a very direct way, but they, too, had kept this a secret. When I shared my model for dream work, others had the courage to reveal their own dreams.

I want this book to help you to organize and explain theoretically what you may already have experienced, and to gain courage to share freely with others the way you have listened and responded to your dreams. I sense that my task is to make acceptable what has been unacceptable. I want you to believe in your dreams enough to share them with others and thus find a new way for God to work in your life.

Using dreams in the therapy process, I have discovered a gold mine of insight and healing both for clients and for myself. I have used some case material in this book to illustrate the message I need to convey.

This is not a scholarly treatise on the subject of dreams. I do not wish to prove a theory, but rather to show you how to experience your dreams. I wish only to challenge you to follow a series of specific instructions and then let the dreams speak for themselves.

This book is a report of the outcome of some ventures into dream work, with the specific purpose of helping people learn to understand the "language of the soul" or, in other words, the deepest part of their existence.

Upon completion of this book, I had a dream that helped me deal with the way I felt about writing it. I will share it as a preliminary example of the way dreams can address a specific concern.

In the dream, I find myself and my wife in a large store owned and operated by a colleague and confidant who is, in real life, a university professor. The atmosphere feels right because my friend is at peace with his task. He is doing what he wants to do and everyone accepts that. The store is in the center of a large city and that, too, feels appropriate.

At some point, I realize that I must not stay here, but must go to a second large building adjoining the store. I ask my wife to come with me. As we enter the building there is an immediate weird sensation—it is filled with hundreds of women, sewing.

Next, I notice they are making all sorts of clothing. These clothes are of patchwork, with the most outrageous colors. When I express fascination with their work, the women are pleased. I decide to purchase one of their cloaks to cover my entire body. The women watch me and again express affirmation. I feel it is the right thing to do. In checking with my wife, she bows out of the decision by simply telling me that I am going to do whatever I want to, so why should she comment. She also says something to the effect that she does not have to wear it, I do.

I proceed to obtain the outfit. I put it on and return to the store. My friend sees it but does not react. It is as if he expected me to buy it. It is late at night as we go out onto the city street. People rush by and pay no attention. I have a feeling that I am dressed oddly, but it certainly makes no difference here. We find our car and return to our home community. I join a multitude of acquaintances and strangers in a variety of public places. At first I notice that people are staring at me. Some are totally aghast; some are confused; others accept my appearance as a novelty. I still sense that the cloak is appropriate. I spend a lot of time and effort explaining its source and its meaning. I tell people that it was made by a group of committed women and had received my colleague's approval. Since they know him, they should understand, but they do not. I feel that a large group does not understand and that my explanation makes no difference.

After awhile I meet a group of youngsters who jeer and mock me. Within, I sense that it is absolutely impossible for them to understand. They are too immature. But if they could understand, they would change their tune. Since they can't, I must accept their reaction. My deep inner feeling at this time is that my cloak has a very profound meaning. Its variety of colors may be different, but they add to its beauty. I reflect on the seamstress who put so much love and care into it. The cloak is significant if one comprehends its meaning. As I face opposition, I am momentarily tempted to flee. I wonder whether I should go home and dispose of my garment, but I do not.

There is such a sense of urgency to make the people understand. They are missing so much by their error. My coat of many colors conveys a beautiful message, but it is too subtle for some to understand.

The meaning of this dream is clear to me. The coat is this book, because that is exactly how I feel about it. I am certain I have discovered a profound truth. It may appear in an unfamiliar form, but I cannot be distracted by that. The "language of the soul" has great meaning for me, and I must continue to present it until it is understood. If some of my audience sees only its absurdity, they have failed to understand its hidden meaning. That is their loss.

I believe the seamstresses were the large group of clients and friends who have affirmed me in writing this book. In reality, these people have been very willing to share their dreams and their prayers to make this project possible. That sense of helpfulness also filled the sewing room in the dream. The women loved me for buying the coat and going out in public with it; they also understood its meaning. In real life, too, there is help and understanding.

My wife's position at the time of purchasing the coat is the same as she has taken in relation to the book. Although she edited, typed, and retyped it, the message I convey is mine, and I have to live with it, not she.

My professor friend has listened to me as I shared my enthusiasm, but he has maintained only an academic interest in the subject matter. He understands what I am doing and he encourages me to live with my writing, even as he lives comfortably with his setting. The store is symbolic of my view of his comfort with his public image. His facial expression in the dream, as does his voice in real life, tells me to live in comfort with my choice, whatever that may be.

The fact that my book should have been symbolized as a coat of many colors troubles me. Is this again related to Joseph's coat? Did it emerge in the dream because of my son's analogy? Or was it because of my childhood when I, too, was penalized for being identified as my father's favorite son? Maybe it is related to the Patriarchal Joseph, in that he was willing to bear the brunt of his calling in life.

After the dream, I must admit to myself the way I really feel about this book on dreams. I believe I have a good idea, provided I am given a chance to present it. If you the reader will stay with me to the end, I believe you also will understand.

I am aware that we are talking not only about the thought level of a person's existence, but about intuitions and feelings—the deepest inner experience of the soul-level of living. This is why we are dealing with such profound truths. Dreams communicate truths from the soul.

Yes, I believe the most meaningful level of a person's existence is the deepest inner self. I also believe it is at this level that we can converse intimately with God and know his personal will for us. The marvelous fact is that this inner self is the source of all dreams, that language of the soul which can help us know and do God's will. Dreams can be used as a source for spiritual growth. They have a way of taking the fragmented pieces of life and organizing them into a simple whole. We are then presented with a significant truth about our lives and given the option to respond. I believe that through our dreams, God is at work in our lives.

Abraham Schmitt

Dreams as Soul Language

1

I have long believed that dreams bear profound messages which slip by and are lost to most people. In fact, a dream has a very personal meaning, meant to be understood and helpful at that exact moment in time. Dreams can be used on a daily basis, as a constant monitor of our position in life.

My belief in dreams is so strong that I think of them as a pathway to the soul, and thus a place to meet God. After this encounter with God, we will know better his wish for us.

It is very sad that many people do not believe, and thus fail to utilize this potential for growth. My purpose is to show you the reader how to make the most of your dreams. I wish to teach you how to go about understanding the "language of the soul."

I had a series of dreams which illustrated to me the way dreams should be understood. The very "language of the soul" was being taught to me as I dreamed. I was not surprised that this should happen, since I already had spent years thinking about and preparing to write about the meaning of dreams. Finally my subconscious picked up the need and began to remind me nightly that I should respond. The less I responded, the more persistent became the dreams. When I accepted their explanation of the understanding of dreams, the dreams ceased. They had, in fact, accomplished their tasks, so there was no need for them to persist.

For the last six months I again have had a recurring dream. I know what it means. But because I have not accepted its message, it returns again and again. I usually enjoy the dream because it is so vivid and at times very peaceful. At other times it leaves me deeply frustrated, but I understand that, too. Therein is also a reward.

The main feature of the dream is a huge underground complex of open spaces. As soon as the dream begins, I say to myself, "Here we go again." I already know what is coming.

One of the spaces is very large and centrally located. At times this is a chapel. At other times it is an enormous cavern. From this main section, there are dozens of smaller openings which also vary in structure from large rooms, or worship areas, to caves. I always have the vague sensation that beyond these are even smaller rooms, each for a different purpose.

Some attributes repeat themselves in the dreams. Each one usually begins with my approaching the opening, which is very small. I always have a strong desire to get away from the outside world by going into this underground space. The way down into it is always difficult. At times there is a narrow passageway with stone steps. At other times I have had to build a ladder to descend about twenty to thirty feet. The entire complex is totally hidden. No one else knows it exists, and I do not want anyone to know. Never is there another person near it or inside it. My desire is to get farther and farther into the complex of rooms, beginning with the largest, and then the next smallest, and the next. There is an understood degree of tranquility, which also begins in the largest and progresses to the tiniest. Only vaguely do I know what lies in the smallest spaces. I am always aware that some are completely empty and very, very quiet. Others have desks and are furnished with writing materials. Still others are lined with books and have a comfortable place to sit and read. Sometimes I am aware that there is also one with a bed, and I sense that tranquil sleep is awaiting me. The idea of worship and meditation is often present. The largest space has, at times, an altar at the far end. One of the tiny rooms is clearly a worship or prayer room.

The one main feature that varies from dream to dream is the distance I succeed in moving into this cavern. I always want to enter very, very badly. But at times I get nowhere. In the worst dreams, the entrance is directly downward and a large stone has sealed it off. My dream then can consist of struggling to try every known means to dislodge it, without success. At these times I awaken distressed, tired, and defeated. The next time, the way in is like an open doorway, and I can readily descend the stairs to the huge chapel. At other times, I spend my whole dream building a wooden ladder which I lower into the hole. It is risky to descend it, but I do it anyway, because of my great desire to go down.

It is fairly common for me to reach the largest opening. Inside, I sense stillness, with never a sound. The altar is always far away. Slowly, I approach it in deep reverence, for I know God bids me on. I also manage, at times, to enter the smaller chapels. Each appears to have a different meaning. Some are brilliantly lit, displaying the most beautiful ornamentation, much of it covered with gold leaf. Others are dark and dull, but symbolize *far more peace. So it is also rewarding to be in those chapels. It is as if my soul is at perfect peace.*

The sense of regret is always present because I want to go beyond to the smallest rooms, but I am never able to do that. They always elude me. I know that and it makes me very sad. When one of these rooms emerges, I want to use it for its purpose—write, meditate, worship God, or simply sleep.

In the sleeping room I have the rare sensation that if I were to enter, I would sleep forever. That feels very good. Since it is so totally quiet and nobody knows the location, there is nothing that could wake me.

The emotional aura surrounding this dream has some distinct repetitions. Yet at times there is a unique difference.

The unifying feeling is very clear. There is a sense of yearning to move from where I am to someplace where I ought to be or want to be. The farther I move, the greater the feeling of fulfillment. The less I move, the more the frustration. I am trying to get away from what is happening on ground level, which is felt as unpleasant, hurried, hassled. The depth has a peaceful air. Whenever I am kept from going ahead, I feel frustration, displeasure, anger.

The differences are experienced as I encounter items in the dream. The long, slow, meditative walk, step by step in the direction of the altar, is very peaceful and satisfying. But then again, it is distressing when I do arrive. The idea of the farthest little room is consoling. When a room comes into particularly clear focus, a surge of creativity, or worship, or meditation fills my being. I always want to be totally engulfed by the feeling, to completely enter that space and remain there. The upsetting feeling comes when I am not able to do that. I am also aware that the venture can end without notice, so I may not really experience it.

I have long ago learned that when I awake from such a dream, I am immediately in a state that is half-way between sleeping and waking. This is the twilight zone. Now I must deliberately tell myself to stay there, for there I shall recapture all the events and the feelings of the dream, and then move toward their application in real life. The beauty of this moment is that I can so naturally and easily move into the unconscious, see all the events and symbols in the dream, and feel the emotions that were attached to each. Just as quickly, I can flip to my conscious level and find those same emotions where they have always been but formerly were hidden from me. It is then a simple step to connect the feelings to the events in life that I have not owned before. Now I have the opportunity to do that and to go one step farther. Since I am now conscious of a new meaning for a part of my life, I ask God to speak to me. In his mercy, I ask him to now reveal the message to me and to give me the courage to respond according to his will.

Let me now analyze the present recurring dream from the vantage point of the twilight zone. I now hear the inner message from inside the dream. It is more like feeling the meaning than conceptually understanding it. The truth is profound, because it is experienced as the deepest part of the self, now revealed.

It is just as clear as when, at a moment of acute loneliness, we know we need someone. It is not a question of deciding whether it is true. It is the finality of truth that someone is missing, and that knowledge results in a response. The dream has spoken from the same depth. It is now that I invite God to speak to me through the dream.

As I flick my view from the unconscious to the conscious, I sense the meaning of the dream. My whole being is yearning for peace. And I hear God saying clearly, "So, act. How can I tell you any more vividly?"

My answer is, "I am trying, Lord, very systematically,

but it is all not very effective." I have spent far too many years getting here, and I have programmed far too many people into my life who will not allow me to act. So the dream repeats itself again and again.

Even now I can recline in a comfortable chair, close my eyes, and descend into the twilight zone; and immediately the scenes from the dream will replay on my inner television screen. It is strange that, depending on my level of mastery of my life situation, the scenes will be different. If I try to replay the dream while the demands of life are too pressing, I get stuck at the entrance to the underground cathedral. Then again, at a particularly peaceful moment, I may even gain the privilege of a slow walk to the altar.

Dreams are built-in monitoring systems that keep constant track of the deepest parts of our existence. They touch on the areas of life that we simply dismiss while awake. Dreams call us to ask ultimate questions about the meaning of our life as a whole, or of a very simple event that we passed over during the day.

For the purpose of clarity, I wish to use my dream trip into the hallowed cavern as an analogy.

While I am on the surface, I am caught up in routine events. In the dream, I am very aware of the deep peaceful cavern that awaits me. In real life, I spend much of my day searching for deeper hidden parts of the self. I am very obviously a believer in the vast unexplored caverns in peoples' lives.

The first striking observation is that the dream portrays a struggle to go from the surface to the caverns below. I believe that is the same ambivalence that I must face in understanding dreams. I simultaneously want to delve into their full meaning, and yet I block my own way. I want to go into the cavern; yet it is my own stone that keeps me out. I am eager enough to work at building a ladder; yet I create the twenty-to-thirty-foot distance that must be crossed. I want to receive the full message of my soul; yet I don't. I want to continue my writing on the subject; but I don't. When one probes the depth of the soul in real life there is a reward, but it calls for a response that I am not always ready to make because of the risk. This dream tells me that, at times, my willingness to understand dreams wins. Then the doorway is open and the concrete steps are finished, and I can go down. At other times the burden of the understanding is too great, so a stone blocks my way.

It is significant that the dream portrays a deep cavern. The term *deeper insight* is exactly what is symbolized. A dream is an opportunity for a deeper trip into the soul. The dream has chosen perfect symbolism. The fact that I go to various depths also portrays my willingness, or unwillingness, to understand the message of my dreams.

By the many caverns, I know the dream has a variety of meanings. The huge central chapel, with an altar at the far end, is the cathedral of my soul. It signifies that I am searching for God's blessing upon my dream venture. In real life, I would like to approach the throne of God and ask him to direct this search. I believe the fact that I do not reach the altar signifies that I have some doubts about my worthiness to go on with this sacred venture. When I reflect upon it in bright daylight, I can easily understand that God is directing me. The dream keeps saying, "Yes, it is within the realm of God's will."

I often enter the smaller chapel. Here I am at complete peace. The writing cavern simply bids me to pick up my pen and write in real life. By doing this I will show that I understood the correlation between the cavern symbolism and the deep ventures of dreams.

I believe the meditation room symbolizes my yearning for a more meaningful life of prayer and silence before

God. It will also help me to better understand dreams and be more effective in writing.

The bedroom scene in the dream signifies ultimate peace. I believe I will only realize this message after the book is finished and I will have earned my rest. I wonder whether it may even signify the ultimate rest beyond life. This would explain why I always have the sensation that it is meant for a final sleep and that I would never wake from it.

So I must leave this area, go back to the remaining compartments of life, and struggle. Then someday the real rest will be mine.

Now, for the purpose of understanding dreams, let us simply visualize that as soon as we dream, we are in the greatest depth of our existence. This is commonly called the unconscious part of the self. I prefer not to use the term *unconscious*, because it has come to mean the frighteningly violent, erratic, aggressive part of the self. I simply do not believe this. When I use the word *unconscious*, I refer to those deep parts of the self where all life's experiences are gathered and filed for later recall. In my analogy, this is the deepest part of the cavern, where there are anterooms that are waiting for me to enter while I am asleep. This is the part of the self I call the soul.

I like to use the analogy of the cavern. It shows us there is surface living, which occupies most of our time while we are awake. It also illustrates that during the dream state we are at a very, very deep level of the self, where all that we hide from ourselves while we are awake exists. Then in a dream we go down, but the meaning is disguised in objects, events, or symbols.

The distance between the two levels is the twilight zone. By twilight, I mean that one's mind is anywhere from fully tuned in to daily events, to totally unconscious.

In the case of a dream, we begin at the bottom. As we wake, we go through the twilight zone and can bring all the new findings back with us as we come to the surface. Most people make this trip rapidly, because as soon as they are awake they want to go on with the events of life. Thus they lose all their treasures en route.

You may not know that the return trip from a dream can be paced at whatever speed you like. You can stop at midpoint in the twilight zone. In this state the imagery of the dream is still very real. The events of the dream and all the emotional nuances that go with every part can be recalled easily. With some practice it is possible to slip farther and farther down into the dream state, so that it actually can be completely relived without falling asleep again. This makes it possible to claim all the gifts from the dream for later use.

To really learn the language of a dream, this art of twilight traveling must be practiced. This will bring to your mind much more material than you would expect.

Whenever I relate my dreams in public, I hear the immediate reaction, "My dreams aren't as complicated as that." My answer is, "Yes, they are, but they must be explored." Most people simply hang on to the parts that were so dramatic they cannot forget them. Then they think that was all there was to the dream. Often, these parts may supply the message of the dream, but 95 percent of its significance may have been missed.

The really important point is that anyone who wants to hear more messages from a dream can simply, at a convenient time, go back down into the cavern and the twilight zone and reexperience many parts of the dream and glean more from it.

One other issue needs to be faced: Why do I use the word *soul*, or even the phrase *soul language*? To me there is no better way to describe what I mean by the deepest part of a person's being. It is the final essence of the self. I believe that Scripture uses the term in the same way. The soul is that part of the self which goes on existing after the body dies. It is the self that will go to be with Jesus. It is the "I" that will live forever; it does not need the body to exist. At this depth of the self, we are most in touch with God, so why not call it the soul? When communication comes from this level of the self, I call it *soul language*.

I have found an interesting insight in *Pastoral Psychiatry: How to Make Psychiatry a Servant of Religion* (1938) by John Sutherland Bonnell, an authority on pastoral counseling. He says that *soul* is really a translation of the Greek word *psyche*. In a lexicon, he discovered these definitions: "Breath, especially as the sign of Life, spirit; The soul of man, as opposed to the body; The soul, mind, reason, understanding." He concluded that the primary meaning of *psyche* is not *mind*, but *soul*. It then follows that *psychology* is the study of the soul, and *psychiatry* is the healing of the soul.

Although the word *psyche* might have been more acceptable, I prefer to use *soul*, which also allows for the spiritual element, the deeper part of the self which makes us uniquely human. It also makes us alive in a special way because God has breathed the breath of life into us to make us "living souls."

Since I believe the Bible is God's revelation of himself, I believe a message from a dream should be interpreted in harmony with the Scriptures. For spiritually sensitive people, the message of dreams uses what is already known about God through the holy Word, but now directly applies to people's lives in areas where they would not otherwise hear it. As soon as the message is heard, even though from another source such as the Scriptures, or by clarification in preaching, or by a sudden awakening, then the dream is no longer necessary and simply will not recur.

Dreams are one way to achieve deeper contact with the

self. At times the message is so crucial that all of life is bent out of shape until it is heard. At other times there is but a small flicker of new insight which may be only amusing. I wish to make clear that when we listen to dreams, we are listening to God.

My Personal Journey with Dreams

2

I have always had very vivid dreams. Over the years I did little with them, other than to remember the most dramatic events. I never systematically explored their meanings or tried to learn their language. My purpose here is to record a series of very significant dreams and show how they helped me gain awareness. I dreamed this first one before I had any real understanding of dreams.

I am in a race, competing with a long line of people on either side of me. I do not recognize anyone, nor do I try to. The whistle blows and we all dash ahead. I am in the lead for a brief period, but it is soon apparent that I am losing the race. I am passed by everyone else. At that moment I become aware of a huge bundle on my back. No one else is carrying a bundle. The more I am aware of the weight, the heavier it becomes. As I am about to collapse, I awake.

A deep feeling of rage engulfed me. It was so unjust! Why was I burdened like that and still expected to compete?

At that time I was at a very precarious situation. I had completed the course work for my doctor's degree in record time, and the next step was the dissertation. Then the drama of life changed. Since I was no longer on stipend money, I needed to find a job. This was very difficult because since I was en route to a higher degree, most agencies did not trust the permanence of my commitment. When I attempted to take a menial staff position, I was told I was overqualified and would be bored. Finally, I managed to find a dead-end, low-ranking, social-work position. To make matters more burdensome, our third child had been born the previous summer and we were expecting another.

I understood that the dream was related to my current problems. The bundle on my back was truly the burden of responsibilities—my wife, my family, my job. The people who passed me were my professional colleagues—those who were not overwrought with responsibilities and could finish the race toward the doctor's degree.

At that time, my response, which I shared with no one, was completely off the track. Secretly, I harbored a great resentment at being saddled with this unfair burden. Without a doubt, I showed my displeasure at home. My error was that I blamed others in order not to be accountable to the message.

The true message was different, and the response should have been different—then I could have received a blessing from it. I could even have made a correct turn at the crossroad.

First of all, I should have acknowledged to myself that I was carrying too much responsibility. Since I could do nothing about much of it, I simply should have accepted it. Second, there was really no race. On the doctoral level, no one is racing with anyone else. Everyone who completes the dissertation receives the degree. There are no quotas. But because I was ahead during the first two years, I needed to prove to my peers that I could come in first in the entire race. The race was in my ego! Here, I should have stopped and said, "I will get there when I get there. At this moment I am committed elsewhere. My family needs my attention. I will get to the dissertation later."

The dream contained a subtle message that the completion of my academic work was very, very important to me, but I could not acknowledge it. The dream implied, too, that my deeper self yearned for that work and felt called to continue. I also missed this message.

In real life, at my job, I wasted much time which I could have used to work on my dissertation. I had been granted all the time I needed for my project.

What did I do at my job? I permitted myself to be distracted by all kinds of mundane pleasures. I was permitted to eat in a very special dining hall where the top professionals met for a several-hour leisurely dinner, served by patients. On the ward where I had my office, I quickly won the admiration of a particular attendant who prepared a special pot of coffee for my desk and kept it hot and filled all day long. Whatever work I did was constantly interrupted by my special hostess or by my sipping of coffee. Thus I permitted myself to feel important.

I missed the point of the dream because I unfairly blamed my family for the problem. If I had owned up to my problem, I would have responded by changing my performance on the job.

Eventually I did finish the degree, but I stayed on in the same position. The attention I now received in the hospital setting was even greater. It was good to be addressed as Doctor all day long. It also fed my vanity to have attendants rise when I entered a room. I thought I was really satisfied with my position. At least I told myself I was.

Then I received an invitation to accept a professorship

at my alma mater, the University of Pennsylvania. At this point, a dream cleared up all my feelings.

The setting is very familiar to me. I am aware that my dreamland is the treeless prairie of Saskatchewan, Canada, the land of my preadulthood years. The exact location is the middle of an open field which covers the entire surface of the earth. Only the blue sky canopy is visible above the surface, a scene very common to that prairie province.

Next I notice row upon row of an unknown crop which extends to the horizon in all directions—roughly a radius of fifteen miles. Then I become aware that I have hoed only two or three rows clean of weeds, and there is an infinite number yet to be done. My back is tired and aching as I rest wearily on my hoe, too discouraged to go on.

Just as I am about to be overcome with despair, a strange automatic hoeing machine drops from the sky to the ground in front of me. It then hoes with lightning speed down one row to the endless horizon. And with equal speed it returns in the next row. In no time, it has completed the circle. As soon as it is finished, it vanishes upward from whence it came. With that, a deep inner peace falls upon my soul. A total experience of euphoria engulfs me.

When I awoke, the analysis of this dream was immediately clear to me.

The weary hoeing was an exact analogy of my feeling about my position at the hospital. This fact startled me to a sudden awareness of how deeply discouraged and near despair I had been. I also felt, on a subconscious level, that there was no end in sight. The position was menial and no matter how hard or how long I tried, it would lead to nothing. I had refused to allow myself to realize this fact. Consciously, I held on to this position which recognized only my master's degree. But I told myself, as I told all others, that it was challenging. I didn't dare do anything else, since my family depended on my little earnings and I could see no way out. The dream told me that I actually felt much differently. In reality, I was suffering deep anguish. The fact that I had paid such a bitter price to obtain the doctoral degree was also reflected in my exhaustion. I now saw that the very bad mood I had often exhibited on many occasions was directly linked to my overall professional despair. Now it all made sense. I invited my dream to speak, and it spoke to me about my soul's despair.

The feeling of euphoria after the magic hoeing told me that acceptance of the university appointment was the correct move to make. The good feelings stayed with me for many years, and I could recreate them simply by recalling the dream. I even used the recall method to dispel fears and doubts about the teaching position. I simply knew that my apprehensions of the moment were superficial, compared to the sense of rightness which the dream had revealed at a much deeper level.

I may even go one step farther and say that the dream was given by God to tell me I was to move on professionally and that he, in his own way, would help me succeed. I had only to trust in him. I often imagined that the machine that came from above was symbolic of God, who, I assume, is able to come down into our lives and intercede for us when the going gets really tough. If we do not see God at work in small things in our lives, then we miss him altogether.

I did go on to teach at the university, until I gradually realized that it, too, was not the end of the road. It was a stepping stone in my growth. However, to call an end to it was traumatic. The next dream, which I had a few months after I left my teaching post for private practice helped me sort out my feelings and gain clarity.

I am back on the university campus. It is all very familiar to me. I recognize all the buildings, which feels good. "This is where I held my professorship," I muse to myself. But I am now dressed in very dirty work clothes, working at rebuilding the brick and redwood pavement around a tree planted on their modern campus. [In reality, I often watched this job being done. All the brick work, the rotted redwood, along with the weeds, must be removed, cleaned out, and reconstructed.] Since construction is a hobby I genuinely enjoy, I am happy in my work, deeply involved and at peace.

Suddenly I look up at the crowd of people rushing by. With twenty thousand students on campus, this was a familiar sight. Then I begin to recognize my colleagues, the faculty members with whom I had once taught. At first, their faces seem very smug, satisfied, preoccupied, self-assured. They seem to know where they are going. As I watch, their pace increases. "They must be going to an extremely important event," I think to myself. Since I recognize them, I begin to greet them. "Hi, Joe!" "Hey, Al! What's the rush?" The first ones turn to look at me. Instead of greeting me in return, however, they appear utterly disgusted that this laborer has the temerity to address them by their first names, rather than by their professional titles.

Then the stream of fellow faculty increases. Their heads are now raised high, their noses pointing upward. I feel intimidated. They now no longer hear me calling them. At this point, I notice that they are carrying identical folders of material that seems very important to me. For a moment I feel that I should go and get a folder, but then it occurs to me that I can't get one anymore. A momentary sense of loss overcomes me. This even changes to dread.

I return to work on my project, and soon I am as deeply absorbed in it as I had been earlier and totally unaware of my surroundings. I am especially careful to lay the bricks very precisely. I feel a deep satisfaction at the creative work I am doing. Slowly the project changes. The work becomes a pedestal which I am now creating out of stone. It becomes more and more elaborate until it seems to be a statue. Everything belongs together in this place. An overwhelming feeling of goodness and well-being overcomes me. "Everything is just as it ought to be—a perfect job. I built it as it should be built. It was my ultimate task and I was obedient." I am saying these words in my dream as I awake.

This dream helped me make a major transition in life. The signals as to where I had come from and where I should be going were very easy to understand.

The first scene in the dream revealed a very distinct sense of loss at what I had left behind at the university. I yearned to be recognized on a first-name basis. I wanted my folder. I wanted to go to the important meeting. I desired to follow my colleagues to the sacred sanctuaries, to do important committee work, but I couldn't. They were even ashamed to recognize me. I could finally admit to myself that I was missing all that, that I was experiencing a loss. It had been a prestigious position, a joint appointment between three departments, involving the training of professional therapists, counselors, and social workers—this in an Ivy League university. I met many famous persons on the staff and others who came as guest speakers and visiting lecturers.

To leave all these people all at once was almost unimaginable. I knew I had won a special place in the lives of a large group of brilliant and renowned colleagues.

They were my friends and daily confidants. It was with them that I tested my ideas and my models of conceptualization. No, these were mine no longer. Now I must allow myself to fully experience the loss.

Next came another painful thought. What about the professional and financial security I had once had?—job security until retirement, with an adequate retirement plan. Does one give this up lightly? The dream told me I did not.

I now accepted that one message of the dream concerned my very obvious sense of regret.

Then I began to see again those haggard faces rushing madly to what obviously was a faculty meeting. Yes, that was exactly what I once had done. At that time I detested the meetings with a perfect passion. Oh, that whole committee game! I was so sick of it. There were hours and hours of endurance tests, where a group of thirty educated human beings pretended to be accomplishing something worthwhile, while everyone attempted desperately to avoid making a decision or doing any work and still leave the overall impression that this was a grand occasion of monumental importance. "Committeeizing," not teaching, was the key test of professorship and departmental loyalty. No wonder those faces were lifted up so high and expressionlessly. They had to be, to endure the next meeting. "Oh! Deliver me even from the memory of all this, dear God," I finally moaned.

Then I recalled the face of my devastated friend whose contract had not been renewed, for fabricated reasons. The awful fear that I might someday fall into that same fate was intolerable. "That's why I quit," I screamed at myself.

At this moment, I wonder why that dream was not a nightmare instead; but maybe I already had resolved the problem sufficiently to have it shown to me that subtly.

I finally came to the concluding scene, and I invited it to

speak to me. Very explicitly, it was symbolic of the new way of life I had chosen. It has been a period of very carefully putting my life in order again, brick by brick. The more engrossed I became in it, the more it rose off the ground into a pedestal and, finally, a monument.

I am totally involved in that process now and, just as in the dream, I feel very good, totally committed to the cause of therapy with couples and individuals, and deeply fulfilled. The deepest message from the final scene tells me I am creating my own destiny. My life, like the form I was building, is now under my own control—to make it what it ought to be. I do not need to call out to passing professors to recognize me and give me a sign of approval.

I then sighed a deep thank you to my God, for I knew I had again heard him speak to me in a dream, as he had done so long ago.

Now, six years later, I am faced with another crossroad. This year I have permitted my schedule to run my life. Each weekday is filled with clients, and weekends can easily be filled with workshops, until no time remains for my personal growth.

I also want to write, but there is no time. Writing gives me a deep sense of direction and a purpose in life as nothing else does. It is not that I mind the therapy sessions. They test my skill to the utmost half-a-dozen times daily. However, the lasting sense of meaning, for me personally, is not there. It is the same with workshops. I believe it has to do with always being available for others' needs, and never for my own. No matter how much I have to offer others, unless it is replenished in some way, it will dry up. Writing is a means of fulfillment for me, but I have no time or energy left.

Then I had an explicit dream which told me it was very important that I reorder my priorities.

I am in the village of my childhood. Next, the very worst farmyard of the neighborhood comes into view. It is as dilapidated and rotten as I remember it from long ago. Just as quickly, a famous author is beside me. He tells me he has purchased this farmyard and would like me to remodel it for his use as an escape and a location for writing.

We can communicate with very few words. Each of us understands the other's thought-process automatically.

He informs me he must escape from eastern Pennsylvania because of the competitive lifestyle, the traffic congestion, and the intolerable rat race he can no longer cope with and also be a creative writer. He says, too, that he must recapture at greater depth his own personhood, which he had lost a number of years ago, and this setting will help him do that. He wants to write a totally different type of book. The new one has to do with himself. He will make an honest revelation of his experiences, instead of observing outer events.

I sense a very intimate awareness of his purpose, and I am immediately ready to carry out his wishes.

It is very easy for me to do the remodeling, since it all happens as if by magic. I only understand what he wants, and then translate it into a construction method. As soon as I begin the task, it is completed. One huge wall of stonework, with a beautiful fireplace, falls into place. A whole new interior emerges. He marvels at my workmanship, but it all feels very natural.

As the interior is completed, together we take note of all the writing areas that he now has available. We experience the new books that will be composed here. The peaceful community, with its rich heritage of caring people, will help him keep in tune with what he has to do. I have a deep sense of fulfillment that I should have been instrumental in helping him leave urban America and come to my village, which he could not have known about *other than through me. I feel very fulfilled and joyful to be part of all this. I have a feeling of wholeness at having completed what I needed to do—of being called to do an important task, whose outcome would affect many people.*

I awoke, immediately certain of my response. I had come back from a weekend retreat only a few days before, very exhausted and bewildered. So I knew I must tie the dream to that real-life event.

First of all, the fact that the author appeared in my dream is obviously the unfulfilled plea to let the author inside me live. And I, too, must escape the rat race and find a secluded haven to write. The dream told me that it was a matter of making a drastic decision; but that once the decision was made, the work would be easy to accomplish. Writing, when I get to it, flows out, just as I waved my hand in that house and a chaotic mess became a haven for writing.

If dreams have such an important message to bring, why then do more people not invite their dreams? Dreams can be used at major crossroads in life to help establish the direction to take and the direction to avoid. Dreams enable one to listen to one's own deepest needs and, at that level, to receive a clear indication of which path to follow. As a Christian, I believe that God leads in this way. Thus life becomes a wholesome emotional and spiritual venture. Because God has used a series of dreams to guide my life, I want others to share my blessing.

P. I. L.

Catch Your Train, Or Else!

3

I am alone tonight. Yesterday at noon I escaped my extremely busy therapy practice by coming to a quiet retreat to meditate, to be replenished. It took me a long time to unwind. A deep sleep did it well. It is from this sleep that I awoke to realize that I had just had another of those mind-expanding dreams.

There is no reason to get up, nor is there any reason to deal with the dream. I remain in my sleep posture, hoping to fall asleep again. I have come here to relax, not to write. But the dream was too vivid to ignore. So without having reached the awake state, I allow the whole dream to float by once more. During this state I am semiawake, or in a deep twilight zone, more dreaming than awake. At this depth the dream is more real than the outer world.

Since I am so deeply involved in writing this book about dreams, I lie here debating whether to blot it all out and enjoy my vacation, or to tap into this one again and see what it has to offer.

At first my original urge wins out. I just do not care to become involved. I want to rest. I have earned it, so let the dream float away. I think of the pad and pencil across the room. If I get up it may interrupt the continuity of the dream, so why bother? That much activity will awaken me too much to remember all its finer details. The twilight state will vanish and recall will become even harder.

I decide I am too tired. I have earned my rest. I do want to do some writing, but not necessarily on dreams. So I decide to turn over and forget it.

But there was something distressing in the dream, and that also makes me want to forget it. I check the time. It is only 6:22 A.M. and I do not need to arise for breakfast until 8:00. So I fade into a state of deeper meditation, and with that, the entire dream is back again in full force.

I now decide to get my pad and pencil. I turn on no lights and open my eyes only enough to see what I am doing. I return to bed and make the following quick notations.

Philadelphia, center city, rushing, dashing. People all over the place, moblike rush hour.
Subway station—bewildered.
I get on—wrong one—I meant to take the Amtrak train.
I can't get off this one.
Frantic.
Must get back to train station on time.
Check watch—too late—too late.
I get off quickly.
I must take train back to station.
Trolley zooms by.
Trolley slows to make corner, stalls.
I get on illegally. I'm so desperate, someone is irritated. I don't care!
I am somewhat relieved.
Now I am really confused.
How will I get home? I missed my train.
I think of my wife and children. How can I tell them?
It's my mistake, not theirs—I feel concern for them.

I can't make them drive 35 miles to center city to get me.
I want to get home so badly.
Home, home—it feels so good to think of it.
There is a train pulling out of the station.
I run beside the engineer, asking if it will stop in the
  suburbs somewhere.
He pays no attention—preoccupied with his duties.
If only I could get to the suburbs, I would save Dorothy
  half the trip and the worst city driving.
I ask every person I meet whether any train will stop in
  Jenkintown? Abington? Willow Grove? They all
  walk by with no response. They mind their own
  business.
I tell them I don't want Dorothy to drive into the city. I
  have four small children. It will make supper late.
  It's too much for the children.
The people don't care. It's just like them.
I am very aware that Dorothy will do whatever needs to
  be done. This feels warm, loving.
I stand on the platform, totally confused, with trains
  pulling out everywhere. Nobody knows how to help
  me.
Everybody is completely dignified and composed as
  they walk by. They know what train to take. They are
  being taken care of. I am the only one who is not.
I'm caring for everybody's needs. Who cares for my
  needs?
This is not the way to do it.
I should not be here. I should be on my train, going
  home on schedule.
There must be a drastic change somewhere.

I awake distressed, restless. I want to forget the dream
and sleep, sleep, sleep.

After the quick outline I have just completed, I go back
to the beginning of the dream again. This time I write it

up in greater detail. Since I am now committed to understanding it as deeply as I can, I will remember more dream material, and also the emotions connected with each event. The dream will give up its secrets to me. It will be especially for me.

As I reflect on the dream, a series of insights flash through my mind.

Just prior to the arrival of the train, when I had plenty of time to catch it, I was walking slowly toward the train station, just as I had done for years. Only this time, people came walking up to me. Some stopped me; others walked beside me, and we were transacting business that was important to them. I was always available for them. I felt important because they needed me. They were my professional colleagues, so I obviously should give them my time and attention. It was actually the preoccupation with these people that made me inadvertently get on the wrong train. My head was with them and not with my own agenda. I did not know where I was "at."

Some time before boarding the train I was engulfed by the center-city rush-hour mob. I ran part of the way. I was bewildered, bumped by the crowd. People were all around. I was soon just dashing past them. There was great confusion around me.

Suddenly I became aware I was on the wrong train and it was already going full speed ahead. A sense of great catastrophe overcame me. I was frantic. I knew I must get off at the first stop and return to try to catch my Amtrak train. I checked my watch, only to realize that the other train must be pulling out of the station at that very moment.

Another new insight dawns upon me now. While contemplating the departing train, in my mind's eye I see more of the dream which I did not notice earlier. My twin brother and a group of his buddies, with attache cases in hand, had walked slowly and directly to that same train.

They had boarded on schedule and were calmly going home as they should, while I was in an underground system, heading in the wrong direction.

There was a feeling that my brother does everything in an orderly way, avoiding all my frantic mix-ups. There was a sense that my brother acts in a simple directed manner, and as a reward, he is going home. In contrast to me, he knows where he is going and what he is doing and does everything the right way.

Next, I realize that I desperately tried to get off the moving subway but could not. I even contemplated leaping off as it was traveling at a high rate of speed. This tells me exactly how desperate I was.

When I finally managed to get off, a second train whizzed by in the right direction, but did not stop. Now I was even more frustrated.

Then a subway surface trolley came by. It had to make some sharp turns, and I ran after it to get on, even though it did not really stop. I sensed the driver's deep displeasure at my behavior. However, he was so engrossed in maneuvering the trolley that he said nothing. I did feel he thought I was a fool. I knew I had committed a violation, but I was too desperate to make up for my error or to care. I really did not wish to be thought an idiot when I was dealing with a crisis like that.

I was somewhat relieved then, since I knew I was at least going back to the train station. It was then that my wife and four children came clearly into my awareness. They would be expecting me home on the usual 6:00 train, but I would not be there. Then I realized that dinner would be ready. They would wait for me, wondering why I was not there. A desperate yearning overcame me, since I wished to be home, where I was supposed to be. Next, I visualized Dorothy packing up the four children in the old van we used to own. She was gladly driving toward the city to pick me up. I needed only to call and tell her where to meet me. She seemed so kind, warm, and willing, even though I was very aware of the huge disruption for her and for the children. Why should she pay the penalty, when it was my error? I had done something wrong. I didn't know exactly what it was, except that I had gotten on the wrong train. There is a gnawing awareness that the error is something more personal, but I can't quite identify it.

Suddenly in the dream I was back at the center-city terminal building of the Amtrak train. There were trains leaving everywhere, but none going to Souderton. Maybe I could take any train to the northern suburbs. That would save Dorothy all the city driving and approximately half the distance. If I could only do that.

It was then that I began to ask people all around me if any of those trains stopped in the cities I named in Lower Bucks or Montgomery county and they paid no attention. They all were engrossed in their own business. They knew where they were going. They would catch their trains, and what I needed did not matter to them. I shouted to them about my plight; I even told them how difficult it would be for my wife and children, but it made no difference.

At one point, a gentleman stopped for one second to tell me that a certain train was going to New Haven. As I asked about the first stop after leaving Philadelphia, he turned and vanished. I dashed up to the engineer of the train and ran beside it as it pulled out, to ask him the same question. He was so busy he was oblivious of me. I kept saying that he did know where the train stopped, but he would not tell me.

Again people were everywhere, rushing by and bumping into me, but always about their own business. I glanced around and noted that many people looked familiar, as if I had seen them before. They were nice people, but they did not care about my plight.

An enormous sense of a terrible wrong overwhelmed me. I thought that if one of them should ask me directions, I would stop to tell them, but they would not do that for me. Wasn't it strange? I'd cared for everybody's need, but who cared for mine, especially when I was in a predicament?

I had the overall feeling in the dream that something is very, very wrong in my life. This is not the way it should be. A drastic change must be made somewhere, for I should never be caught in this predicament again.

I must do something. It is a far bigger problem than could be handled there on the railway platform.

Immediately upon waking, I am in a state of distress, a huge internal upheaval. It is too big to face, so I really want to run from it—not face it, but fall asleep.

At the same time, I have the feeling that there is an answer in this dream that I must not let pass by. If I do, I will miss an important message from my soul. I must stop and listen to it.

I wish to pursue this dream. It hounded me last night, and now I shall hound it until it gives up its secrets while I am awake. You see, I am ready to hear what I need to hear, and I am ready to respond fully. Actually, the overall message is so obvious that I at this very minute, by the act of writing, am already obeying.

Now I will go back to the dream material, back into the twilight zone, so as to reexperience at a deeper level the greater meaning in the dream.

The reentering of a twilight zone is an art that can be learned. It is very easy for me to do that today, since I am still alone. I cannot be disturbed, because nobody knows where I am. My surroundings are very important to me. Even the fact that I am near a telephone that could ring and distract me is a major disturbance. Here, that is not possible.

I close my eyes as I reflect and allow the dream to float

by, again and again. Parts touch me deeply. I make a mental note of these as I go on in a state of solitude.

Suddenly four clear impressions strike me. These result from my feelings much more than from my thought process. However, for me to remember them, they also must be rational. I believe my soul is now speaking to me and I am listening.

This is the order in which these four thoughts came to me.

1. *You are not where you should be.* Running around frantically in a center-city railway, when you should be home, is lunatic.

2. *Dorothy and the family pay a penalty for your lost state;* but they are willing to do that. Sure, dinner would wait, and they would drive all those miles to rescue you wherever you are, but that is such a needless thing to do. It is not the real answer but only a temporary solution. So what is the solution? Well, get on the stick, pay attention to what you are doing and "catch your train."

3. *You are available to everyone who asks for you.* Why did I dawdle down the street, meeting the need of everybody who stopped me? Of course they had a real need and I was the person to ask. I could help, so why not help? At this moment, I remember looking at a number of passersby in the dream and thinking, "You look familiar. I think I once helped you." Even the engineer had a familiar look, as if I had looked into his eyes once before. Maybe it was that he once asked me for help, not the other way around.

4. *Everyone else is totally indifferent to your need.* No matter who I asked, no matter how desperate I became, nobody—but nobody—responded to my request. People bumped into me to get where they were going, but never aided me on my path. The people I asked for information didn't even show the courtesy of looking at me. The

engineer and the trolley driver went about their business. But what about my business? Does no one care?

As I played back these four issues, suddenly a tilted square came into my vision, and the four items were listed at the four corners. In the middle of the square were these words: *confusion, despair, bewilderment.* The center of the square took on a spiral form, going down and farther downward. More distress, more helplessness, more lostness.

I suddenly sat up and shouted, "O.K., Abe, account for this!"

Now I could feel the emotions flowing through my body, and in my usual fashion I began to pace back and forth. I believe I release disabling energy in this way and can then begin to focus my effort in a productive direction.

In order not to lose my discovery, I drew the square so that one corner would point to the top of the page and the opposite corner would point downward, as Illustration 1 shows.

I put the most important statement in the upper corner: "You are not where you should be"; on the right side, "Dorothy and the family pay a penalty for your lost state"; at the bottom, "You are available to everyone who asks for you"; to the left, "Everyone else is totally indifferent to your need." Then across the top of the page I printed in bold letters, O.K., ABE, ACCOUNT FOR THIS.

Now I must make the crossover into daily life which will give me the message of my soul and the appeal to respond. By now I am so deeply involved in my dream and have such openness to my life and inner voices, that it is easy to decode what I did and felt in the dream. It is very similar to a major aspect of my present routine daily life. The dream is speaking to me, and now is the time to listen, understand, and obey.

If I really face the demand to "account for this," it is simple—"Abe, you are missing your train of life. You had

Illustration 1.
The Diagram I Made to Portray the Message of My Dream

O.K., ABE, ACCOUNT FOR THIS!

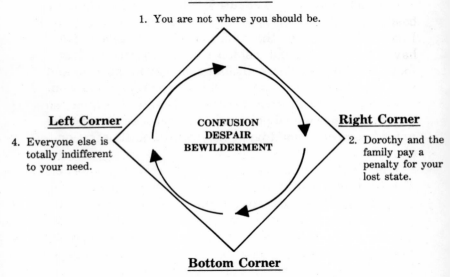

Top Corner

1. You are not where you should be.

Left Corner

4. Everyone else is totally indifferent to your need.

**CONFUSION
DESPAIR
BEWILDERMENT**

Right Corner

2. Dorothy and the family pay a penalty for your lost state.

Bottom Corner

3. You are available to everyone who asks for you.

Catch your train, or else!

better own this fact and do something about it, or you will continue to suffer confusion, aimlessness, and desperation and run around frantically in wrong directions. You may never get where your soul, or may I say God, is calling you to be." I boldly write across the bottom of the page, CATCH YOUR TRAIN, OR ELSE!

I can easily tell where I am supposed to be. I am to write this book on dreams, as well as other books. If I don't do it now, I never will.

Am I certain of this? Yes, because as soon as I touch base with this fact, I have peace in my soul and with God. I have heard the "language of my soul" in a dream and I have obeyed.

A dream is given us to help us understand an important message and then to enable us to make a change in our life to synchronize with that message. A dream is meant for growth.

As I acknowledge the message of the dream, I have an overwhelming sense of awareness, joy, and fulfillment.

Now I want to explain the final stage of learning the "language of the soul." You can go back to the same dream again and again and allow yourself to be touched by it and gain more and more insight. A dream is like an onion—you can peel it layer after layer, continually coming nearer and nearer to the center of your being.

It is also true that you can have other dreams that use different symbolism but continue the same message. So if a person becomes weary of one dream, only a nap later, a new one can emerge that will provide a new drama with the same message, but approached from another direction.

A day and a half later as I continue the dream work, I consider each of the four corners of my square and indicate my response, beginning at the left corner.

Why do I feel that people in my immediate environment are indifferent to my need? Who are these people?

The first group that immediately comes to my mind is made up of my spiritual brothers and sisters in the local church and the church at large. Because of my doctor's degree and since I am known as a therapist, they keep me in that pigeonhole and will not let me out. My dream tells me I am weary of this and need to be rescued from it.

My response is that I must nurture those few relationships which let me be me. I hear clearly that I shall move on that one.

The next group that rushes by me—people concerned only with their own needs—is my current caseload of eighty couples and individual clients. Since I believe so devoutly that therapy is a one-way relationship, this cannot be changed. These people purchase my undivided attention, and they have a perfect right to be indifferent to me. I am startled by the one client in fifty who even greets me with, "How are you?" A quick "Fine, thank you" is all such a person wants. If I sometimes, for the sake of variety, answer by telling how I really feel, I can see that is not what was meant.

My soul is telling me I must own this condition, but there is a penalty. This type of one-sided relationship "goes with the territory," but I must respond to these relationships, too. Otherwise, while I am being so devoutly professional I am damaging my soul. My group of clients will soon become like the mad crowd rushing by at the railway terminal—only a sea of faces.

As I move to the bottom corner of my square, I believe I can answer what the other corner left unanswered.

How available must I be for everyone in this world? The dream tells me that I have overdone it. I must redefine my priorities and then act upon that decision, or else I will "miss my train."

In the dream, people come one after another, asking questions, detaining me, engaging me until I am so distracted I lose touch with where I am going. The "language of the soul" says simply, "You keep this up and you will receive a rude awakening, but then it will be too late." When I wake up, I am like Scrooge waking to find that Christmas yet to come has not happened. I am still in the present where I, like he, can make my changes now and thus divert the penalty.

I also know, as the dream indicates, that I gain a great deal of pleasure from being needed. The slow pace of the people around me in the dream was enjoyable. Herein is the trap. I enjoy my work, so I give every calling client an appointment, even though there is no vacancy in the schedule for the next month. Stepping back just a little farther, I know I don't really need to be needed. There is the lurking notion that as a child of the depression from the windblown Saskatchewan prairie, at some very deep unconscious level I still see myself as the poor little farm boy in a situation where it was impossible to provide a livelihood for our family of ten. I will make an effort to find a solution for this theme later.

In the meantime, my response leads me to the next corner. There is my Dorothy, waiting to be called upon to bail me out when I get into predicaments way over my head.

In the dream, I saw her driving the van in the direction of Philadelphia. She had somehow managed to feed four children and get them into the vehicle. I could see the driver's seat from miles away. She was smiling and driving down a local road, coming to get me. She was ready to rescue me, even though the predicament was of my own making.

So the message of the soul says, "Listen to Dorothy more. Let her tell you what to do. She really is ready to help with your life predicament."

First of all, she is completely ready to handle my office schedule differently. Since she already does all the scheduling, she crosses out segments that are to be left vacant. All I have to do is to leave them vacant. When I take a call with a desperate scream for help, I write an appointment right over her reserved spot. I capitulate again to being the rescuer of all mankind. This whole issue must be turned over to her and her decisions should be final.

I hear another voice in this particular issue. Dorothy is also my editor and typist. I believe the symbol of the train and my need to be on it are directly related to my writing. Dorothy is waiting to be handed my written manuscript. When I write a chapter, I am answering the ultimate plea of the dream. The instruction to be at the place where I ought to be is a clear-cut call to complete another book.

The most beautiful happening occurred during the last hours. The focus of the whole book has come to me very clearly and that, too, is a gift from God.

Prior to this, I was repeatedly overwhelmed, wondering why I should write another book. But the dream conveys the feeling that I have a special gift to offer. This book is not to be an elaboration of theories about dreams, nor of research on dreams. However, I do have an ability to listen to hidden messages, to open up the secrets of the heart. I must write a book that, through both style and content, will lead you the reader to the wellspring, so you can drink from it and be made whole through the understanding of dreams.

Now I have also answered my upper corner question: Why am I stuck in the dream where I was not supposed to be? Why could I not reach the place I was destined to be? After a whole day of writing, I have finally obeyed my inner light and followed it through to the finish. I shall dream that dream no more. I have heard the message and obeyed.

A response must be made to each dream, or the pleading voice will come back repeatedly.

I will respond to this dream. It is very clear that for me to "catch my train," I must write. I cannot let the clutter of a therapy practice and the pressure of the many calls for help distract me. If I acknowledge all those calls, I will miss my own calling. And if I miss my own calling too long, I will become emotionally emaciated so that I will not be able to respond to the needs of others. This dream contains a very urgent appeal.

I also believe that God is present in the plea for me to respond, that God is in touch with my soul—my innermost being—because I have asked him to be present. God is speaking to me through each dream. It is my option to respond.

Now that I have returned to my home and several weeks have passed, I can reflect on the meaning of that dream in connection with my writing. The zeal to continue has not left me. I have written chapter after chapter. Everything is so very vivid: I know the theme of this book; I know the impact I want it to make. There remains only the matter of compiling it in the most effective way. I am pulsating with creativity. It is as if I have found a well within myself that is supplying me with endless water to nurture this task. I hope you, too, will be nurtured by it.

Steps for Understanding Dreams

4

In order to understand the meaning of dreams, three separate states must be recognized: the *awake state;* the *dream state;* the *twilight state*. Each has a very distinct role in the dreaming process. While awake, we pursue the routine requirements of daily living. At times we may be very aware of the deeper levels of our life processes. However, since life has so many demands, many of these important things must be passed over. That they are not recognized does not mean that they are not a vital part of our lives. When we fall asleep these same missed messages are translated into analogies in the form of dreams. During the waking-up process we go through the twilight state, in which we are still in touch with what happened in the dream, but we are also entering the fully awake state of daily living. We make this cycle one or more times every night.

If we are to capitalize on the messages of our dreams, we must understand and respond to each of these phases with the greatest awareness possible.

These are the steps for understanding dreams.

Step 1. Failure to Hear and Respond to the Message of the Soul

Dreams originate out of a need that has not been met. Let me hasten to say that it is impossible to meet all our needs. Each moment of life creates more needs, even as others are being met.

Some needs come out of childhood. When we were young, when everything took on such enormous importance, we may have been hurt by intentions, by the events of life, or by the inadvertent behavior of our peers or kinfolk. These scars and bruises may remain for decades, waiting to be examined, healed, and then laid aside.

The mystery of daily living also creates needs. We cannot know the full depth of things that happen to us, so this leaves a void that needs to be filled.

I like to think God is calling us to live more and more meaningful lives. Sometimes we do not hear his voice clearly because we are caught up in the daily necessities of living. When we do stop and listen to him, we may not always fully understand his highest and best intentions for us. There are always deeper and deeper mysteries to be heard. In dreams, God can lead us to some of these mysteries.

At other times the needs in life are so obvious that we can hear the message as often as we care to listen, though we may not know how to respond. There are also occasions when we simply cannot respond because these needs are in direct conflict with other more urgent ones. At such times we sort out whatever we can and do our best, knowing full well that much of what is begging for recognition in our lives must be neglected.

Every day the process of filling the reservoirs of the soul with uncompleted tasks, with unheard messages, with distorted responses continues. Then a deeper psychic mechanism goes into operation—the dream.

Step 2. Symbols and Events in the Dream

As an individual goes into the dream state, one or more messages of the deeper life are dramatized in symbolic form. This experience is an analogy of what was missed in earlier living. The dream drama takes on a symbolic form, so as to effectively communicate the full meaning of the intended message. Symbols are selected in a strength equal to the depth of the message to be conveyed. If a person has been frightened by a near-drowning incident, the danger of drowning may be the central theme of years of recurring dreams, although the person has no fear of water and may even be an excellent swimmer, as the dream in chapter 7 illustrates.

Do not pay too much attention to the symbols and events of a dream. They are only the form by which the message is conveyed.

Step 3. Emotions in the Dream

My experience with dreams shows that the symbols and events do not carry the most important part of the message. Instead, the meaning is best conveyed by the emotions in the dream. It is as if the dream attempts to clarify its message in two ways. The first is by way of the plot. At times the meaning may be completely incomprehensible, but at other times, very clear. The feeling experience in the dream relates the meaning more closely to real life. It appears that the intention of the dream is to do all it can to tell the dreamer what it is trying to say. Yet the dream does not reveal the explicit message.

As I help people learn the "language of the soul," I find they begin to step back, even while dreaming, to observe the events and the feelings, and then can fully interpret the meaning as part of the dream itself.

Dreams are left at a nebulous level so that we are free either to understand them or to forget them. There are many dreams that one is simply not ready for or not courageous enough to understand. One may be given a

Illustration 2. Steps for Understanding Dreams

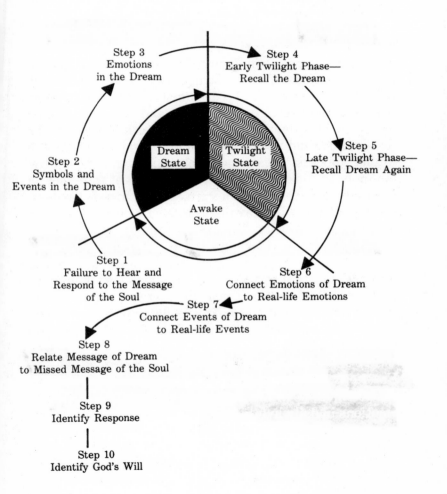

signal that there is an important message, but the psyche may not be up to dealing with it. The emotions may be so veiled that one senses only distress when one awakes, but has no idea of the meaning.

As people grow emotionally, especially in therapy, these same messages become more and more clear until they can be understood.

Step 4. Early Twilight Phase—Recall the Dream

It is best to replay all the events and emotions in the dream as you are coming out of the dream state and are barely conscious. This is usually easy to do because one actually can return to the dream state. First the major events in the dream become clear, and then they can be arranged in sequential order. As one thinks about the dream, finer and finer details fill in the gaps until the full drama appears. Next, each segment is related to the emotions in the dream. It is very important to reflect on precisely what these feelings are. What you recall and put into words now will be available later. If you fail to do this, a memory can easily slip away into oblivion.

Step 5. Late Twilight Phase—Recall Dream Again

It is best to bring the dream back with you from the unconscious state as you wake. It is also very helpful to write out all the material in a quick scrawl, even if it is in simple words and phrases. An excellent method would be to use a tape recorder and record audibly whatever you have experienced.

Step 6. Connect the Emotions of the Dream to Real-life Emotions

The emotions in the dream are the key link to similar emotions in daily living. When we make this connection, we have reached the height in the art of dream interpretation.

At a recent workshop I included the theme of dreams—the language of the soul. A pastor's wife tuned in on this particular emphasis—that the emotions matter more than the events of a dream. She excitedly told her husband, who decided to note his dreams carefully the following night. He even chose a particular issue which he wished clarified. When he awoke, he could readily recall the dream, but it just did not make sense. His wife pressed him to recall the feelings that were present. He was able to do that. Then she showed him that by using the feeling route, he had an answer to his request. He was startled by the clarity of his answer and also by how revealing the dream was. The wife was so delighted that she shared the incident with me.

Step 7. Connect Events of Dream to Real-life Events

If you have completed the feeling connections as indicated in Step 6, you will readily make the connections with the events.

Step 8. Relate Message of Dream to Missed Message of the Soul

As you play back the events and feelings of the dream, you must keep your mind open to the areas of your life to which you may have failed to respond. In Illustration 2, I identify this failure as Step 1. The danger of making a faulty connection is so great that I have devoted a whole chapter to it (chapter 5).

Many of the examples show how to make the connection between the dream and its meaning in real life. Some critics of my theory fear this connection could be made randomly, and thus a dream could mean what you want it to mean. I do not believe this is the case in reality. If you very deliberately play the dream back, both in the twilight stage and in the awake stage, it will be clear that there is only one meaning, and it will be the right one. Your inner harmony will simply verify that it is the true meaning. This takes practice. One successful experience will convince the skeptic. Try asking for a specific message for a specific need.

A friend once heard me talk about the theory of dreams.

She entered into the discussion with interest, but dismissed it as not having much worth for her. It seemed too farfetched for her to use; she assigned it to others who were more enlightened than she considered herself. Then she heard me say, "You have to work at it." This phrase kept returning to her thoughts. Earlier, she had assumed that meaningful dreams came only to special people and had concluded that she was not one of them. However, if it was a matter of working at it—that she could do. She must only trust what I had been talking about and try it.

On our next visit, she gave the following account, which I recorded. I use it with her awareness.

"I have never experienced dreaming as I did after I heard you talk about it last time.

"I did exactly as you told me. . . . I was doing dishes and I said to myself, 'What really bugs me in life? What is a real problem to me? What is something that I don't know how to solve?' And there is something I don't like, that really bothers me.

"After some contemplation, I knew there definitely was a problem in my life. I knew exactly what it was. I wanted help to see why I felt like I did about this area of life.

"I had no answer to my question. All I knew was that I had decided I had a problem. I also prayed that I might find an answer, and if God could speak through a dream, I was ready to listen.

"That night I got my answer in a three-part dream. Three different scenes. They are so clear to me even now.

"After I woke I again did just what you said to do. After the dream, I lay in bed real quiet. I kept my eyes closed. I went over and over and over the dream. I analyzed it, applied it to myself and the situation I am in, which I had defined the night before. The more I thought about the dream, the more things applied to my problem. I got more out of it each time I went back over it.

"When I got up the next morning, I said to myself, 'Oh, that was no great thing. It was a very ordinary dream.' It did not upset my life as I thought a dream should. It did not change my life particularly."

Now she raised her voice as if to make a very important point.

"It gave me an answer to an area of my life where I had asked for help and it told me what I badly needed to hear. Now when things happen that are related to that problem, I just go back to that dream, and I say, 'Jennifer, you remember that last scene!' And it is right there before me, with my answer. It's just so neat! It really is!"

Dreams do respond to the asked for or unasked for missed messages of life.

Step 9. Identify Response

A dream demands a response, or else it is useless. Sometimes the response is simply to own the fact that a problem has been clarified, but that nothing can be done about it. However, "owning" a problem *is* a response. At times the response may require therapy to follow through on the deep emotional need that has been identified. At other times, it is simply to do what the dream told us to do.

Step 10. Identify God's Will

I do not believe a dream has really been used unless we take the message to God and ask for help. I like to use the apostle Paul's question, "What will you have me to do?" when he had a real confrontation with God on the road to Damascus. Ultimately, we need to ask several questions: What is God's will for me in the light of the dream? How can I respond in a way that will bring glory to him?

The one step that the chart does not illustrate is the practice of "twilight meditation" during any of the five awake states. This means that you may return to the dream later in meditation and can then reexperience the twilight phase. If you are able to do this, you can bring many more details into play and receive more insight.

The diagram clarifies the entire dreaming process and its relationship to real living. In summary, it says that dreams originate in the deepest part of the inner self, which I call the soul. Dreams are the result of unmet needs. We may have failed to recognize or take into account something that should be noticed. There may be very beautiful aspects of our lives which we simply have failed to accept, perhaps because we feel unworthy of the affirmation. Therefore a dream emerges to call our attention to that beauty. More often, dreams are caused by personal failure, areas of our life that need attention but for some reason have not received it. Many times we are too busy with surface matters and do not have time for hidden concerns.

I would like to believe that God can be the source of dreams for spiritually sensitive people. He is present in our deepest inner being, so when a call comes from that depth, I think it is spiritually healthy to say God is calling. If he is calling, we need to hear and respond.

The dream itself is a very explicit way to dramatize the intended message. It comes in visual and auditory, as well as emotional form. The selection of the drama is always appropriate to the depth of the message. Much that occurs in dreams comes from our past, but in a dream it is exaggerated so as to arouse a profound emotional reaction.

As we wake, we can examine the crucial issues that are plaguing us, while cycling back into the twilight zone to gain more meaning from the dream. This type of grappling with one's life—in the context of the dream—will gradually bring an awareness of the primary message of the dream and its meaning for real life.

I must emphasize that a dream's message comes from

within. As a result, we must search that inner dream world, then move to the outer real world to find the meaning of the message for our life today.

I have often visualized a dream as a letter from my soul, written with disappearing ink. As it is being written, it is as clear as the drama and the emotions of the dream. But at that time I am asleep, so I cannot read it. In the transitional state of waking, the writing will vanish. So I must read it as often as possible before it is gone, and then rewrite it with permanent ink. Here the dilemma is that if I write too much, the invisible ink vanishes before I am finished. I must read the letter again and again so that I can get the entire message before it is gone, and yet at the same time, record it for later use.

Once it is written on paper or in the memory, then it can be utilized for growth.

False Understanding = False Interpretation

5

It is very easy to read the signposts in a dream incorrectly. I now wish to wave a warning flag. It is not unusual for friends to approach me with a pleasant grin as they say, "Heh, Abe, I dreamt about you last night." The anticipated response is, "Aren't you pleased and honored to appear in my dream?"

What I would like to say is, "No, I am not honored, because it says nothing about me. It only says something about you. Depending on what I symbolized in your dream, it may tell me how you feel about me." If I do pursue the inquiry, they are too embarrassed to tell me the answer or the dream.

During the past year our daughter has had a recurring dream. It is so terrifying and so vivid that she calls it a nightmare. The dream began immediately after she graduated from college and has continued until the present time.

She always finds herself back in college, with all the familiar scenery and people. A sudden terror befalls her as she realizes that she is not as current in her studies as she had assumed. Instead, she is a full two semesters behind. The thought of this enormous amount of uncompleted work which she did not know was unfinished overcomes her with dread.

There was no solution as she awoke trembling. Several weeks later the same scene recurs.

She did not mention this dream to anyone until we raised the question of graduate studies a week ago. Then she told us the dream and commented, "I can't go back to school until that terrifying nightmare goes away."

By implication she meant that her college education has left a hidden scar that must heal before she can consider further education.

She shared this dream with a college classmate recently. Her friend immediately responded that there had been no indication in college that she was being bruised by the experience. Together, they concluded that actually, she was a great procrastinator—often projects and papers had not been completed until the absolute deadline. Even then, there would be several incompletes to catch up on in the next term. But as a whole, she felt very confident that she had easily mastered the material, with a lot of time left over for social events. Surely there was no cause for such a deep scar.

I spent several days reflecting about her dream. Then I concluded that her interpretation was completely erroneous. The dream was saying nothing about her past college experience, but was concerned with her experiences during this past year. She completed college as a very promising social worker but was unable to find a job in the field. After months of searching she did find work which, at first, appeared much beneath her.

I concluded that the dreams were telling her to wake up now. "You are falling behind in life." Since her two younger siblings have higher aspirations, there must be an obvious sense that she must get going or they will leave her behind. Unless she acknowledges this and does something about it, she will someday have a rude awakening.

Since I was deeply involved in writing about dreams, I shared my interpretation with her. She stopped me to tell me she had just had a sequel and that I needed to hear it first.

It was late fall of this year and in my mind I was absolutely sure that I had been awarded my diploma a year ago. Classes had started and I had to meet a lot of prerequisites. I couldn't back out because the tuition was paid. I worried about the money, since my brother had just entered another college. To tell Mother about the cost distressed me greatly. For awhile I tried to figure out who to confront to talk to about it. I was just certain it was a mistake.

Finally I went to the registrar's office and asked to have my credits tabulated. They discovered that I had met all my requirements and already had the degree.

Then I decided to stay to complete the course work. I would have fun doing it. It was not required but, since the tuition was paid, why not enjoy it? A deep sense of peace came over me as I awoke.

This dream was so clear that when she woke, she was sure she was in college.

Now we mutually decoded both dreams. She accepted the validity of my interpretation of the first recurring dream. The latest did not end where the others did, but went on to a resolution.

This was exactly what has happened to her during the last several months. She had decided not to go on to graduate school, but had done her job so effectively that it had grown far beyond her anticipation. She has earned much affirmation and admiration from her employer. She may not be in the field of her college degree, but she is using it in an effective and satisfactory way. A sense of inner peace has come over her, assuring her that she need not dread the future.

Her latest dream was telling her that, on her own, she has resolved her vocational life and has had fun doing it. "While you are in it, you might as well enjoy it," is the final message.

Most people assume that there is a simple direct connection between the symbol in the dream and the events in real life. To make this kind of connection can be disastrous, as I shall illustrate further with a dream reported to me by a participant in a workshop.

Lynn, it's Lynn. He recognized her immediately as she stepped out of nowhere into his dream. He had last seen her thirty years ago. And here she was again, just as beautiful and as gorgeous. All his yearnings for her returned in full passion as if he were sixteen again. The fear that she would reject him or turn away, just as she had done so long ago, lurked in his mind. His first surprise was that she came directly toward him. Pure joy overwhelmed him. She came closer and closer and the ecstasy increased. The whole universe was bathed in light. There was music everywhere. He felt beautiful, courageous, and right, as he asked her to dance with him. Her response was, "I would be delighted. I've been waiting for you, Tim. Where have you been all these years?"

He could remember only that he had been unavailable for some reason, perhaps far away. But he did not answer because the reason was too vague. She touched him lightly as they began to dance. The sensation of completion, fulfillment, and total wholeness was penetrating his entire being as he awoke.

He remained motionless, refusing to open his eyes, as he recreated the events and feelings again and again. He wanted the dream to be true now. He clung to every feeling, every sensation, as long as he could. "It can't go away. I need that blissful feeling of being totally loved so desperately. I must have it. I must have it." Some of that ecstasy stayed with him for days afterward. He could recreate the feeling simply by meditating on the dream and on the real events that had happened so long ago.

Tim had grown up on a farm where everyone was committed to hard work. His father was cold and aloof as he often labored silently beside Tim and his several brothers. They were a very religious family, their piety rigidly trained and faithfully obeyed. Tim felt inferior, shy, and doubted his self-worth and popularity as a high school student. His excellent grades and diligent studies gained him recognition from his elders, but he doubted his status with his peers.

Lynn! Yes, he had known Lynn, but for a long time only in fantasy and from a distance. She was far too popular, too beautiful for any possibility of courtship. Then at one school dance, she had approached him and, much to his astonishment, agreed to remain his partner for the evening. She accepted another date, and Tim's yearning for her was a reality. For three months they went steady. The girl he once could admire only from across the room was now his and his alone for dates and, yes, even a few kisses—the very first romantic kisses of his life. His whole existence had reached the height of his greatest fantasy.

But just as suddenly as it had begun, it ended. She simply moved on to the next boy. Tim sank into a pit of despair from which he did not recover for six months. He did not date again until college, when he met, dated, and finally married his present wife. The euphoric experience was conspicuously missing, but he would not risk that again. He now dealt with the selection and dating-mating process more realistically and carefully.

Their twenty-five-year marriage had been equally practical and very, very dull. It was a loveless life that neither seemed to have the energy or ability to turn into a true meaningful relationship. So they gave up and endured.

And then this vivid dream had brought back a memory of all that could have been, all he had missed. If only he had not been destroyed so early, he would have been able to truly select a mate for love and have the passionate years of marriage he deserved. At least, so he thought.

When he could hang onto the dream no longer, the thought of his real life and real wife came back to him. The contrast was too much to take, so he turned to confront her with a depth of feeling he had never shared before. First he told her the content of the dream with eloquence. Then he proceeded to tell her how much Lynn had meant to him and that he had selected a wife who was far from his first choice. He also retold the story of their marriage in terms of his extreme despair, discouragement, and futility.

When his wife attempted to discuss the situation— especially the fact that he seemed to be saying that she was the wrong person for him and that the years of a mediocre marriage were her fault—he fell into an uncontrollable rage.

The weeks that followed were indeed very sullen in that household. The wife knew their marriage was far from fantastic, but there definitely had been very good periods. Finally, she found it very difficult to accept that the problem was all a matter of mismatching.

Tim was confused by the whole situation; the memory of the feelings in the dream and of the experiences so long ago still occupied his thoughts much of the time. It also distressed him to realize how devastated he had been afterward. What did that say about him at this stage of his life? And what has he been dumping on his wife?

He decided to make a secret pilgrimage to his home state to see what he could learn about Lynn. A business trip provided the perfect occasion. It was easy to find Lynn's widowed mother. She welcomed him. She remembered his family, but very little about him. He learned that Lynn had married the fellow she had selected after him; that several children who were now grown had been born. The marriage had ended after about eighteen years, and Lynn rather quickly married a divorcé who had enthralled her to the degree that she was willing to hurt everyone for this new man. The aged mother could not understand and still grieved the loss of what she thought was an acceptable marriage. Lynn's second marriage had ended only recently. Now she was back in the community, living alone. The mother was sure Lynn would be very eager to see him, since she was exceptionally frustrated at this time. At the urging of the mother, he called Lynn, and they met at a nearby restaurant. The thought of seeing her now as a divorcee caused him a lot of stress. His memory of her was very vivid. Yet he had a very deep personal agenda to settle. What had he missed in life? And could he have had it with Lynn? Could he find it now, by meeting the person whom he thought had contributed so much to his downfall?

Upon meeting Lynn, Tim's letdown was so great that he shared very little about himself—not the aftereffects of her rejection, not even the dream. His only pleasure was that he was now very much the stronger person in this relationship. So he knew he could drop his fantasy forever.

When he returned home, the confusion of the dream, his reaction to it, and his wife's waiting aloofness were too much.

He knew of my interest in dreams, so he asked to talk to

me. My most effective intervention was to help Tim correctly interpret his dream, and then do something different with its meaning, with his life, and finally, with his marriage.

His error was that he saw his dream as an unconscious wish-fulfilling experience. I rejected this theory, as most therapists do today.

Tim needed to know that his dream spoke from the deepest innermost part of his present life. It was a symbolization of meaningful material that had been hidden from his awareness. The dream was an attempt by his unconscious self, by means of gently passing fictional characters and scenery through his mind, to call to his attention something he has not allowed himself to admit. A past event was used only to clarify the present situation.

Once Tim began to really explore his life, he could very readily admit to an interesting pattern.

The early years of young adulthood and marriage were essentially as he had perceived. He had experienced deep feelings of inadequacy as the result of a childhood which had left very little room for his discovery of a positive self-image. He had carried this attitude with him for years; it was also reflected in his difficulty in establishing a relationship with his wife.

He had failed to own a very significant factor which explained the message in his dream. Approximately ten years before, he had begun an inner journey toward personal fulfillment. Since by vocation he is a college professor, he pushed ahead in his own education, completed a doctorate, and was promoted. He also had commited himself to good teacher-student relationships that brought him much personal reward.

When Tim finally was able to recall that he had been asked by his professional colleagues to deliver a major address at a convention, I followed a hunch. I wondered about the timing of that occasion and the dream. A little figuring resulted in his conclusion that they had occurred at approximately the same time.

With a little prodding, Tim began to recall more material in relation to the convention speech. When he first saw the printed program, he was overwhelmed by the famous persons who would also be speaking. Worst of all, they would all be hearing him, too. The old feeling of inadequacy returned—especially the stage fright which he had battled for a long time. Then he remembered his early years in teaching, when every lecture brought on anxiety. As years went by, he had mastered this stress, until now he enjoyed his class presentations and did a great deal of public speaking. But never had he faced such a prestigious audience.

However, he had gained victory over the fear. As he prepared his material, he knew he had something very significant to say; otherwise, he would not have been asked. Besides, why could he not be himself? It was not a life-or-death issue. A general sense of his own competence had returned as he took his place at the podium.

Upon completion of the speech he had received much acclamation. Many people affirmed him for his performance. He left with the impression that it might even have been the highlight of the occasion, as some individuals had insisted.

It was shortly after this that he had had the dream.

I asked Tim about his understanding of the dream. He quickly used the expression "a wish-fulfillment yearning."

Then what did that dream mean in those terms?

"I understood it to mean that I was desiring to be married to my girl friend of sixteen years ago and that I was enraged in my deep unconscious because my wife and I had such a shallow marriage. I blamed her, because my real self was prepared for the significant marriage the dream portrayed."

At this point I helped Tim redefine the meaning of dreams as I understood them and showed him how to accurately interpret the dream he had experienced.

I told him that dreams tend to be set on the stage of one's childhood or developmental years, since it is during those years that life is experienced most intensely. It also indicates that a dream deals with very profound material that most people do not permit themselves to experience in adulthood. The childhood scene is recreated in order to give it scenery equal to the depth of the message, so that the dreamer, if willing, can understand the full meaning. This was why the scene of Tim's dream was set at the adolescent dance.

I continued by telling him that the purpose of dreams is to help a person discover a very profound message about the deepest part of the innermost being—a part the person has not as yet permitted him or herself to be aware of or to own—not "wish fulfillment," as Tim had assumed. Dreams are the psyche's desperate attempt to heal the dreamer. It is as if the inner self wants the person to be whole, to put a finger on the most meaningful struggle, the greatest hurt, or the most significant psychological achievement.

The problem is that the individual often cannot bear to hear this message. It may be too painful or, at the other extreme, too positive. It is as if we refuse to listen to the most important messages about ourselves. It could be that to discover life's real meaning would force us to make changes that are too great. Personality change is frightening.

Thus the need for dreams. The unconscious, using persons and scenery from long ago, replays life's drama, in symbolic form, before the eyes of the sleeper. Whether to discover the meaning of the dream and respond to it, or to let it pass by with a few residual sensations and no response, is left entirely to the conscious mind while fully awake. Dreams can tell us the real truth about ourselves. Then it is our option whether we really care to know or do not wish to know the message.

Fortunately, the unconscious is not easily dissuaded. Dreams will be repeated again and again. Sometimes the same dream will recur regularly, until it becomes so familiar we already know exactly what will happen next. We may, even while we are dreaming, anticipate the events as they were in an earlier dream.

The recurring dream will stop as soon as the individual stops rejecting the message and honestly hears it as it correlates with present experience. The persistent unconscious will finally win, and the individual will be the beneficiary.

A dream can be a therapeutic experience that does not cost anything.

Now Tim interjected. "How, then, should I interpret my dream?"

"Tim, I do not want to do it for you. I know you are impatient. But you will be better off if you can do it yourself. Let me give you more explicit directions, so that you will not only understand this dream, but many more in the future.

"The first step is to recall the facts as accurately as possible. Do not allow any outside reality to enter your mind at the moment of waking. To do this, simply keep your eyes closed and play back the events of the dream over and over. The very first thing is to get the facts of the dream clearly imprinted in your conscious mind.

"The next step is to get in touch with all the emotions present in the dream. Exactly how did you feel about each person and each event? It is absolutely essential to focus even more on the complete emotional content of the dream than on the events, in order to accurately take the next step.

"Then, very cautiously, return to reality, but to your

emotional reality, rather than to events. Somewhere in your existence, you do have the feelings that have just been duplicated in the dream. It is usually very easy to do this, because the feelings in the dream are precisely those you are now struggling with. If you are ready to face the real ones, you will know!

"The first stage is to ask the key questions: 'O.K., so what does that say to me?' And then, finally, 'What should I do, now that I have gained this brilliant ray of insight?'"

With this, Tim was ready to claim his insights.

"It was very apparent that this dream had nothing to do with my present marriage, or with the person Lynn. My first course of action is to tell my wife, and very, very penitently, apologize. I also want to tell her about my trip to find Lynn and my rude awakening.

"Actually, if I am really honest with her, I will tell her our marriage has been quite fulfilling for me during the last ten years, and she needs to know that. I will even tell her that I think she presently excels Lynn, whom I now believe was rather pathetic. The path of her life is obvious. Had I in fact married her, I would probably be the divorcé I have often wished I were. Only she would have divorced me. I had better drop altogether the fantasy I have cherished for so long.

"The dream told me to admit to myself that I really do feel very good about myself—that the old inferiority, and even the feeling of defectiveness are gone forever.

"Also, I now understand why the dream was set on the dance floor where Lynn and I met. The feeling I now have about myself is exactly the same as the feeling I momentarily captured when Lynn accepted me as her date. If she believed in me enough to love me, then *I* could love me. I have returned to that same stage of life. Only now it is for real.

"The fact that in the dream Lynn accepted my

invitation with such enthusiasm, in contrast to her cruel rejection in real life, is obvious to me. For years, I believed that her rejection was the most important fact of my life. I felt I was not worthy of being accepted—primarily, by myself.

"I also now know that the origin of this feeling began long before I met Lynn. In a family of four boys, with me the youngest, and as indifferent as my parents were to our feelings, I had already incorporated a fragile self-image. Lynn's rejection finished me off.

"What am I going to do about it? Well, first of all, I am going to celebrate myself as a person—my life's journey—and rejoice over the victory. I will remember the dream forever. Then, the homework with my wife is obvious."

His final remark was, "Isn't it strange how I used the dream as ammunition to take a pot shot at my wife? I used it for my own purpose, rather than letting it tell me the truth about myself."

It is very easy to make false interpretations of dreams. It is wrong to assume that only the events in the dream contain the real message. This illustration shows that events cannot be taken literally. To assume that dreams have prophetic proclamations is also completely out of keeping with my belief in dreams.

Foretelling of the future is still very closely associated with dreams in the minds of most people. This view causes people to avoid working with their dreams, because it seems so mystical, even weird. As a result, most people totally miss the meaning of their dreams.

Then there are those who simply state that they were directly called by God through a dream. They may make a broad proclamation about themselves and their call, or about the future. I think, this, also, is a faulty association.

At a public meeting some years ago when I used a

dream to illustrate a point, I was confronted immediately afterward by a very frustrated mission board executive. He told me that their board had been bombarded by a man who claimed that, through a dream, he had been called to foreign mission service and was to be accepted by their agency. In his recurring dream, he would always take an airplane from his home community, fly to the city where the board had its headquarters, and then to a specific country in Africa. The board reviewed his credentials and found him unacceptable on many counts. When the applicant was informed of this, he was sure the board was going against the will of God. He insisted they were to send him to Africa as a missionary. He even threatened to publicly proclaim his frustration at the mission board's spiritual blindness. In final desperation, the executive exclaimed, "What shall we do with him?"

I was very quick to tell the delegate that the man's interpretation of his dream was erroneous. He had assumed that dream events are to be taken literally, which they are not. I immediately surmised that the applicant had very likely had a major emotional and spiritual awakening, which was symbolized by his plane trip to the mission field.

I was then told that the applicant had elaborated in great detail about his great personality change. I recommended that the executive explain to the man this new understanding of his dream, encourage him to own the meaning of his newly discovered zest for life, and respond appropriately. Then the message of the dream will be clear. In no way did the symbolism of the flight mean that the man was to be on a plane. The representative was greatly relieved and seemed confident that the board now would be able to deal with the situation.

Dreams Can Give Specific Directions

6

Dreams can accomplish a very specific purpose in your life.

Before retiring at bedtime, you can ask for a dream to clarify an issue you are struggling with. There is a probability that a dream that night will answer it.

It is best to spend time meditating on the issue. Think of the alternatives. Think of the unresolved facts. Think of your feelings, and anything else that may be related to the subject. Then confidently go to sleep, with a prayer on your lips that God will visit you that night with an answer. It is really that simple.

When I taught at the university, I frequently asked a class of students to follow my instructions on dreaming. Invariably, one-third of the students would come to class with a dream they had dreamt the night before.

Since many of them failed to be very clear on the issue they wanted clarified, they usually found it hard to relate the dream to the real-life concern. They also had difficulty understanding the dream events, since they simply did not trust their intuitive process to help them reach the deeper message. However, of the several students who followed my instruction precisely, each usually came up with a gem of a dream. These convinced the greatest doubter in the class that dreams are far more within a person's command than is generally assumed.

Here is an occasion when I requested a dream with very specific directions and I received an answer. We were in a mountain retreat center where I was the only resource person. One hundred fifty people had registered for the event. The topic concerned my recent book, *The Art of Listening with Love.* My task was to assist these very devout, dedicated people—people who had come from many states and provinces to listen lovingly to themselves and to others. As usual, there were beautiful events. Individuals gained spiritual and emotional insights. Many made new commitments to be fulfilled in their lives and to be fulfilling for others. The task of leadership weighed heavily on me, since the responsibility rested on my shoulders.

We had already had the introductory Friday night session and three very intense Saturday meetings. It was the end of the day, and I was to give my final input before bedtime. On Sunday morning there was to be only one morning session before the end of the workshop. I wanted the last event to create a climax and closure to the entire weekend, so that the whole experience would have maximum benefit for everyone involved. I was particularly concerned about the fact that the group was so large. Many had traveled hundreds of miles and spent hundreds of dollars to be there. So my own sense of adequacy as a leader was also a factor. I then shared all these concerns with the group and told them about my theory on dreams. I suggested that tonight, they ask to dream. I, too, would ask God to visit me in a very special way, to reveal to me how I should conduct the Sunday morning session so that it would achieve its intended purpose. I even told them I had a rather high degree of certainty that this would happen. You see, that's how confident I am about the notion that dreams do occur upon our request—and that the content can be focused upon a specific subject. And above all, that God will speak in this way.

My entire request was granted, and when I shared it the next day, the group was amazed.

I will say, also, that about one-third of the group had asked for a dream, and much to everyone's surprise, the dreams were very explicit. For some, the content was exactly what they had requested.

Sharing all this made the morning worship experience very special. God seemed so real and so very near to many of us.

Before I reveal my dream, I want to list those things that were my deepest concerns at bedtime.

The first was my personal adequacy to conduct the workshop. It seemed that there were too many people, expecting too much from me. At times like this, my peasant beginnings in Saskatchewan tend to surface. Most of the audience had grown up in middle- to upper-middle-class America. At times the gap between us catches me off guard. Rationally, I am aware that I have excelled academically and professionally, but that success does not always sublimate the emotions involved.

Second, I am concerned that I may create another gap. There is one thing I have to watch carefully. I become so carried away with my journey into the inner emotional experience that some persons are offended that I do not properly recognize the spiritual dimensions. So I asked very specifically, in my prayerful plea, that I might also meet those needs.

Finally, I do want my calling in life affirmed. I personally feel very strongly that I am called by God to carry out a mission, and if possible, I wanted the dream to underscore that. It is clear to me that helping persons with emotional problems is my calling. The troublesome part is that I am very successful in doing this, and that does not always fit the conventional definition of a Christian calling.

So, with ample prayerful reflection on the above issues, I yielded to God in sleep. My dream the next morning answered my request.

The dream opens with a clear awareness that I am a guest consultant at the Temple University School of Education. I feel very much at home, as if many persons know who I am and what I have to offer. I am a bit startled at this knowledge, but that is overshadowed by the overall sense of anticipation about what I am about to do. Next, I realize I am not in education per se, but that is all right, since they need me to add a new perspective to their school. Even though I am outside their field, they want me to go much deeper into the experiential aspect of teacher training. There is a clear sense of this difference, but it feels good.

Next I find myself in a large auditorium, giving an address on the subject of my book. Students and faculty are eagerly listening. More and more faculty members slip into the room, as if anxious to catch every word. I have several sensations: a personal feeling of phenomenal achievement. People are being helped and pleased. Students and faculty frequently interrupt to ask very specific questions and offer amplification with profound insight. Some doctoral candidates receive flashes of inspiration for their dissertations. I trigger more and more conceptualization among faculty members, which blends into the whole phenomenon as they rise to share it with all of us. A feeling of extreme acceptance, gratitude, and wonder fills the room. The fact that I facilitated this happening is obvious. I feel that I am coming at the subject from an entirely different perspective, and this is why the meeting is so stimulating. It is a wonderful experience.

There is a momentary pause as my credentials are checked. Someone is of the opinion that I am a charlatan, that I received my doctorate from a mail-order university. When it is made clear that this is not so but that it came from an Ivy League university, laughter fills the room. There is a sense of absurdity, but this is quickly followed by an affirmation of authenticity. There is a feeling of my being an imposter versus being genuine, but the latter wins out and they are grateful. Peace engulfs the situation, and I feel good.

Suddenly high officials, including the university president, arrive to escort me away. We walk through a whole maze of hallways, rooms, and foyers. I have no idea why this is happening or where I am going. We go through another door, and we must pass through the two-room shack of my childhood. The place is still as barren and bleak as it was then.

Soon huge, gaping, rotten holes appear in the floor. We must walk around them, since we are still going somewhere else. I am ashamed. I apologize and try to explain about my past. I tell them we were very poor. The house was old and rotting and we couldn't afford to fix it. They listen carefully and are moved by my feelings. They say they don't mind. I sense that the holes are all right. They are mine. I own them. The others accept them, even though they are completely unfamiliar with such sights. A feeling of complete ownership of my past life predominates.

Soon we are passing prestigious offices. More and more important people join the procession, and we finally arrive at the very best office—the office of the president of the university.

Now the real purpose of my being here is unveiled. They had scheduled this entire event to offer me a professorship at the university. I very naturally decline, because I have other far more important work to do, quite a distance from here. A very, very deep peace and acceptance sets in. There is no struggle or discussion, because they understand. They just wanted me to know that the invitation was there. However, I must obey my calling.

We return via the same passageways. The rotten holes in the floor are even more conspicuous now. I have a mixture of feelings. I wish I hadn't been reminded of them and that they hadn't seen them again. However, the same acceptance prevails.

Then we pass a long line of students and faculty. I am repeatedly asked, with much anticipation, if I accepted the faculty position. They are saddened when I tell them I did not. They respond with affirming statements which repeatedly contain the words honesty *and* integrity. *This implies that they understand—that these words describe my highest priority in life and that they admire me for it.*

A deep sense of my need to do what I have to do in life takes precedence over the university's offer. I must leave to do it, to whatever place that might be. At times they were bewildered by my need, but again, yielded willingly.

I am overcome with a deep feeling of gratitude for their affirmation. My visit had far more than met their expectations.

In the final moments, there is a very warm farewell. It is formal and dignified, befitting such an occasion. I then go on my way, which is the correct thing to do.

In the twilight zone, as I was slowly waking, I felt fulfilled and comforted. I was deeply in touch with my inner experience. I could play back the entire dream as vividly as I had experienced it initially. I also knew, with absolute certainty, that my bedtime request had been answered.

Then I made the following statement. "My call has just been affirmed. I have to be about my Father's business, and I now know, more than ever before, what that is. I cannot let anything, any invitation or temptation, sidetrack me from this."

I now should define how precisely my dream fulfilled my request of the previous day.

The focus I needed for the Sunday morning workshop was available. I simply helped the group work through all the dreams they wanted to share, as well as my own dream. They enjoyed doing this, since the material was personal.

The most profound result was the knowledge that we had asked specifically for concrete directions the night before and had received them. It felt as though God were right there with us. Why should he not, since theologically we all agreed that he was present and working in our lives? That it should be so precise was difficult for some to believe.

The really good part of this experience was that it enabled almost everyone to become effectively involved in the group experience. That was exactly what I wanted for closure. I did not want to do a formal presentation, which is often necessary when the group is not sufficiently motivated. The dream experience triggered an explosion of spiritual excitement. At the conclusion, we shared the holy Communion. As we turned heavenward, we sensed a deep unity as one Body of Christ that had already lived that unity.

The nature of the dream allowed me to do several things. I really needed to share with the group my personal struggle to know God's will for my life. This was especially necessary since I was going to tell them that this would be my final seminar at this location in the foreseeable future. They very clearly understood that the central message of my dream was that I must be "about my Father's business." In the dream, they and the many previous workshop participants were really the audience.

It was clear that I had to say, "No, no more workshops." This was painful both for them and for me.

This very workshop had become an annual tradition at the retreat center. There was no question that it had been successful. Many people came back year after year. Some brought or sent their troubled friends, to help them find a new way of relating to each other. It was this very increase in interest and size that made the entire retreat too much for me to handle. Each year more and more troubled people came. Many should have been in therapy instead. However, they still expected me to accomplish in three days what, in an office, would ordinarily take months.

They could also understand the fact that the university group, in the dream, knew that I had to say no. They knew that I believed God had told me to keep my focus very clearly on my overall goal, no matter who made what kind of offer. So in the end, I bade them farewell for the indefinite future, even as I had in the dream.

In the dream the conspicuous dichotomy between my humble origin and the prestigious offer of the university also had some valuable insights for the group.

They understood immediately why the house of my childhood, with those huge rotten holes, should appear. It was very obvious that I was still struggling with my past. They wanted to know a lot more about that past, which I freely shared. I wanted them to take me off an exalted pedestal and allow me to be a human being. Then they could better deal with their frailties. Earlier, they had felt that, with all my education and experience, I was a breed apart and that in the end, I could not understand their struggles. But now they knew that I could and did identify with their shame and sorrow, for I had been there too.

I could honestly admit that the honor they bestowed on me felt very good, just as it had in the dream. I received an affirmation that was really uplifting and would inspire me to continue, even though I could not fulfill their yearning for my return to the retreat center.

Yes, I do believe that we can ask directly for dreams that point us in the way we should go. We can then trust the answer and accept that God will speak very specifically through dreams. Then we must follow, and he will bless our obedience.

I have not returned to this retreat center for additional workshops. Actually, I have terminated most speaking assignments. That dream gave such a clear answer that I am convinced that therein lies my purpose. I do not need to debate that subject further. God spoke in a dream, and I heard and obeyed.

Dreams Demand a Response

7

A person dreams because something is not right in his or her life. When some change is necessary but unrecognized, a silent messenger arrives at night to prod the sleeper to awake to a new style of living. If there is no response, then the same dream can reoccur literally dozens of times. For some individuals the symbolism changes each time, although the message continues to urge correct understanding and a response.

Sandy's history illustrates the persistence of a dream, and also how precisely the message can point to the problem that needs to be solved. I will introduce Sandy by quoting from the journal she kept during therapy.

The following note appeared in her journal after an early session.

April 22. Hi Journal!
  I feel great this morning! Last night I had a headache like you wouldn't believe. I tried to figure out what was causing it to make it go away. But I think the reasons were too many and complex. Looking into myself, like I do in therapy, stirs up many deep and strong emotions, even ones I'm not aware

of, that are causing hurt. Anyway, this morning I feel wonderful—health does mean everything.

It should be noted that a whole variety of psychosomatic illnesses had brought Sandy into therapy. Her headaches were only one symptom. Others were tightness in her neck, rapid deep breathing, clenching of the teeth, and a terrifying fear of supermarkets.

Getting back to the purpose of this chapter, the first journal entry showed that Sandy could not figure out what was wrong with her. But she needed to do that in order to find healing. The reasons, she said, were too many and complex. Three nights later, she had a vivid dream which revealed that the reason was very simple and singular. However, the response was very difficult.

The journal entry shows that Sandy really wanted to know what was wrong with her. She is very highly motivated. So in a few days she was rewarded by her subconscious, which gave her a gift of her problem in symbolic form. On May 5, she brought the written dream to the therapy session. She proceeded to read the following statement.

April 25—Last Night's Dream.
Events: (in the dream)
   We went to Wildwood, New Jersey, for the day, to swim in the ocean. The waves were huge, the undertow was very strong.
   I wouldn't go in very far. My husband and some other people were out past the breakers on rafts—blue and green. All of a sudden there appeared a pumping machine and some men trying to pump out a body. A guy had fallen off his raft and been caught in the undertow. They found him—his name was Zachary.
Feelings: intense fear of drowning—I woke up believing that perhaps I wouldn't go in the ocean ever again.

I asked Sandy if she had any idea what the dream meant, and she said she did not. The name Zachary bothered her, but it, too, had no meaning.

After a little more reflection, she added, "As long as I can remember, I've had scary dreams about the ocean. I have a great fear of drowning. The undertow bothers me very, very much."

At that moment she shuddered all over and gasped for air. She had allowed herself to enter the dream again emotionally, and a violent reaction followed.

Most people will pursue the dream no further than she did: "I am afraid of the ocean so I should stay away." They assume that this was the message of the dream. Yes, that was a key part of the dream. However, Sandy already knew that fact consciously, so no dream was needed to tell her that.

It is like entering a cavern. Sandy has taken only a few steps down, then stopped. The key to dream work is to keep on going, down, down into the cavern, and collect gems all along the way. It is best to gather as many beautiful jewels as possible from any one dream. One should be free to claim whatever it will release. Not to do so is like starting to enter the cavern, catching one glimpse of it from the entrance, and then running away, saying, "That's all I want to see," although you know the cave is hundreds of feet deep, with myriad side tunnels, each with a beautiful scene of its own. Most people stop exactly where Sandy did and thus miss all the mystery waiting to unfold through the dream.

I valued this experience because Sandy had permitted herself to enter the twilight state of the dream, even while she was in the office, and replayed the drowning scene. She was especially aghast at the sensation of the undertow. "This is important," I told myself, "and I must return to it later." It was too frightening at that moment.

Her shudders were an explicit way of getting rid of the thought. It was too painful now.

Remember that my goal in therapy was to go with Sandy down the twilight stairs of the cave, to whatever depth she could go, to gather the precious subconscious material we would find along the way. But one of the rules is that I can go no faster or farther than Sandy. Whenever I received a signal, like the shudder, then I paused until she indicated she was ready to go on.

Sandy looked at me very intently. She was exploring my response. I could exhibit no fear, but confidence and trust, for she depended on me. I could not panic, even if she did. I communicated that I would show her the way if she became lost. I would also bring her back to the surface if she reached too great a depth.

After a moment of silent communication, she went on. "You know I have had dreams about the ocean all my life. Sometimes I am in a glass house on the ocean front, and huge waves are pounding against the glass. I am fearful of the undertow, which I know is strong, and I am frightened, hoping it will not catch me.

"In most of my dreams the waves are small, but the undertow is always strong. What really bothers me is that in many of my dreams I barely put my foot in the water, and the undertow grabs me. Then I have to grope at the beach to keep from being carried away. It seems so completely unfair. At very bad moments in the dreams, I simply put my foot in the water and out I go, swept away. Then I wake in complete terror."

As soon as she arrived at this point, she again shuddered at the depth to which she had permitted herself to experience the dream. Now she was grasping her neck with both hands cupped around her chin, as if her head needed to be held up. This was obviously a very intense moment for her.

I paused again to wait for a signal from her that she was ready to go on.

One thing needs to be said about Sandy. She is boldly and courageously pursuing awareness. She may momentarily retreat when the experience becomes too overwhelming, but then she sits up again and is seeking more meaning.

"I don't exactly understand why I relate to water the way I do. I am a good swimmer. I learned to swim long ago and have always enjoyed it. Then why the terrifying ocean scenes in my dream?"

At this point I ventured, "I assume you know that the meaning of this dream is more personal than simply the fear of water."

She diverted that insight, as if it would be better to find a meaning that had to do only with water. She then told of an experience while water-skiing as a teenager. She had fallen off in a very dirty and fast-flowing river on the West Coast. Before those in the boat could pick her up, she had been completely overcome with terror.

She had no sooner said this than she decided that this event could not have been the source of her dream, because the dream had preceded the incident. It had begun when she was a small child and had been repeated so often that she knew the exact sequence of events even as she was dreaming. The only unknown was how far she would be swept out to sea. Or would it be fatal this time? She was always relieved to wake, knowing that the ultimate end she dreaded so much had not happened.

Next she recalled having been told that as a two- or three-year-old, she nearly drowned in a swimming pool. She was found floating in the water but, with only slight resuscitation, had been revived. She also dismissed this event, since it had happened before she was consciously aware and she now knew about it only from being told by others.

Here she wanted clarification as to whether there was any relationship between these events and the dream. My view is that the only connection was in the symbolism. I believe the ocean-drowning scene was the scenario for the dream because the incidents she described must have been so terrifying. In order for the soul to speak its language to her, it had selected an experience that would be capable of carrying the needed depth of intensity. It was saying that a very powerful message needed to be conveyed. That is why the event was so powerful and why it had been replayed during all twenty-seven years of her life.

She immediately asked, "What if the two incidents had never occurred? Would I have had the repeated dream?"

I told her, "Yes, I think you would. The only difference would be in the scene—it would not be water. The subconscious would select the next best scene, with the same message, because something needs to be heard that you have not heard. Your soul has a message for you that you will not listen to. Yet it must be heard now!"

Sandy eagerly asked, "Well, what is it?"

"I believe you have a hunch about what it is trying to tell you. Let me illustrate the dream in a diagram and retell it. Just allow yourself to reexperience it at whatever depth of emotion you can."

I began drawing ocean waves across the page, illustrating the breakers, and also showing very clearly that they were coming toward the shore (see Illustration 3).

Sandy stopped me to say that often the waves were not that large.

I caught the message. She did not want to deal with the big waves first. She wanted to face the more calm ones.

So I began again, telling her that the waves are now much smaller and slower. I also drew them slowly so as to keep pace with her stress level. Then I drew the diagram, as if it were a cross section of the ocean. I emphasized the shoreline, the beach, and then the sloping ocean floor.

Illustration 3. The Symbolism in Sandy's Recurring Dreams

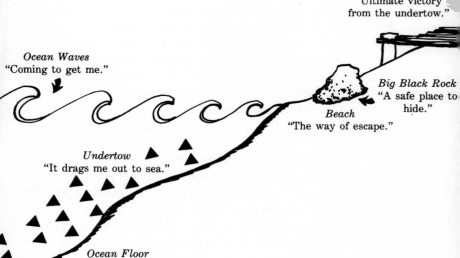

Boardwalk
"Ultimate victory
from the undertow."

Ocean Waves
"Coming to get me."

Big Black Rock
"A safe place to
hide."

Beach
"The way of escape."

Undertow
"It drags me out to sea."

Ocean Floor
"To the endless depth."

After only this much, she gasped and again clasped her neck.

"Shall I go on?" I asked.

"Yes, go ahead, I'm O.K."

Then I diagrammed the undercurrent moving along the ocean floor out to sea. To illustrate the intensity of the flow I drew a lot of arrows pointing away from the shore, down the sloping sea bottom, and out to greater and greater depth.

Sandy reacted violently to this. Her neck and face broke out in red blotches, as they have done for many years, causing her much embarrassment. Next she held her head, saying she felt faint and light-headed, the main reasons she had sought therapy. This led to headache. In spite of all these symptoms, she was not about to stop. She wanted to go on and on.

Sandy was, at this point, deep into the twilight zone, where every scene in the dream was being reexperienced as if it were happening now. She was also close to the real-life events being symbolized, because she was, after all, fully awake. And in this case the security of the therapy experience was facilitating the process.

I asked her to simply blurt out exactly what she was experiencing right now. With that, the words started to roll like the waves.

"I feel I am losing control, overwhelmed. I am being pushed by a powerful force into an unknown sea. I can't control it or stop it. It has hold of me and I have no handle on it. I am scared. I am afraid. No, even terrified. It is even a choking feeling, as if I will not be able to breathe. I am drowning."

I asked her in what substance she was drowning.

"I am drowning in fear—the fear of completely losing control. If it keeps on going, there will be no end to it. Death must not be the only end. That is what is so frightening.

"Oh, now I know. The waves are any event in my life that can hook me into being a slave to that event or person. As soon as I am hooked, the undercurrent takes over and sweeps me out to sea. I lose complete control because other people or events take control of me and I can't stop it, no matter how hard I try."

I asked why that was so.

Her response was instantaneous. "Because I have never felt that I was a good person. If anyone wants anything of me, I must go along with it, because I feel so worthless that there is nothing in me to stop it. No matter how wrong it is for me. If I have no say-so over my life, I can be swept away by anything or anybody, especially if they make me feel guilty for not doing it. Guilt really gets me. I will do just about anything if someone puts a guilt trip on me. Afterward, I hate it. I hate myself for having done the exact opposite of what I wanted, or what was right for me, but I had no control. And the worst feeling is that all this is going to get worse until heaven only knows what the outcome will be. I will have no self at all, and I will be helplessly a victim of everything and everybody else.

"Emotionally, an experience like this is so frightening. It's like dying, but not being dead. Just dying and dying, and yet having to live so as to die and die again."

At this time Sandy was exhibiting all the physical symptoms again. She was hiding the blotches and even had pulled up her knees as if to curl up and vanish.

Sandy exhibited enormous strength as she went through with this entire scene, but in a moment she was back to grappling with the real issue.

"This is perfectly illustrated in my relationship with an eighty-three-year-old widow whom I have been visiting off and on for the last year, after her husband died. I wanted to be a good Christian and show her I cared. So I began dropping by and phoning her occasionally. Sometimes I could coax her to go out to lunch, but more often she just wanted to stay home.

"At first I enjoyed our visits. I had chosen to do what I did, so I felt free. Gradually it turned into an obligation, and I began to resent her. She subtly communicated to me that I was expected to call and visit her every so often. Yet she never wanted to call me or accept my invitations to come to our home. It was a one-sided relationship, and that really bothered me.

"Yesterday I had this strong compulsion to go over to see her. The guilt for not going was worse than the helplessness of being near her. So I went, because it was easier.

"As I got close to the house, my head became light. I felt faint. I sat in her living room, supposedly visiting with her, but my head was in fog. I was preoccupied only with what will she make me do and how can I get out of here. I have lost my freedom completely with her. I managed to leave, but it took twenty minutes to get from the chair to the door and another ten from the door to the car."

I asked, "How is this related to the dream?"

"Well, she is like the waves, and in her case it could be very small waves. All I did was take one step into her ocean, and then the undertow took over and I became a victim again. It's all very simple. The waves are the events in my life. They can be big or little, that does not matter—anything that hangs an obligation on me; any situation I step into where I suddenly can't get out. Then the undercurrent takes over and I am swept away.

"Do you know this happens every time I walk into a shopping mall? I become flushed; I feel hot and terribly self-conscious, as if my body were exposed to people; and then I panic. It is so bad that at times I fear I will faint and drop to the floor in a public place."

What was really the source of Sandy's problem? It is

best described by Sandy herself, in an illustration she gave. As a child, she would follow her father around, just to be near him. Often while he was working, he would pass the hammer to her to hold. She spent many hours holding the hammer or other tools. She did this to evoke recognition, gratitude, and affection from him, but they never came. She was then already aware that she did not particularly care to hold the hammer, but was waiting with that unfulfilled yearning. It became more painful when she realized that he never caught on to what she needed, but instead assumed that she liked to hold the hammer. "Dad would always thank me, but that wasn't what I wanted. I wanted to be close to him, to know him, to have a mutual bond on a feeling level."

She had realized in an earlier session that she does not have the self-esteem to "drop the hammer." She is still waiting in vain, ready to do anyone's bidding. If only she could have her emotional needs met in return. But as soon as she reaches out, rather than her need for affirmation being met, she again becomes caught in the other's need and lacks the courage to escape.

After that session Sandy wrote in her journal:

April 22

I didn't get back to this yesterday because of a bad headache, and I didn't feel like writing. That statement "I am still holding the hammer" just came out of me in therapy. I often remember the hours I spent helping Dad—just to be near him. I longed for his love and companionship. He was so special to me. Yet he would never share his inner self with me, and still won't. I guess I feel as though I'm still holding the hammer, because I still yearn for his love and approval. I hold on to the hope that some day he will slip up and let down his barriers and let me in. But I don't think he ever will. Instead, I need to put down the hammer. . . .

I love you, Dad.

Sandy is responding and must continue to respond to the message of her dream. Once she emerges to a certain level as a person, which the dream is especially urging her to do, then the dream, which has repeated itself for twenty years, will finally go away, never to return to haunt her.

Sandy's most general response must be to permit herself to feel she is a lovable, beautiful, and acceptable person. She must feel this without anyone else needing to say it to her. To possess this level of self-esteem will enable her to feel that she is not dependent on others' affirmation, but can trust her own inner resources.

As a searching, believing Christian, Sandy makes all this a matter of daily prayer, asking the Lord to touch her ailing body, to quicken her mind, to give her insight. She also begs to have her heart opened to new experiences, even though she is afraid. She seeks God's direction in the whole therapy process so that his will may be done there.

Sandy knows she must take more risks in life, even at the expense of great discomfort. In the latest session, she told of having seen the movie *Ordinary People*. She wished so much that she could have the freedom of that young fellow in the therapy hour—that she could get up, walk over to another chair, or just walk around in the room. When I asked her to grant herself that freedom today, she froze on the spot. She just curled up on the sofa, terrified. But then she suddenly sprang to her feet and boldly took a rocking chair, rested a moment, then ran back to her spot on the sofa and exclaimed, "There, I did it."

We have now identified the "waves" and the "undertow" as the two dragons in her life that must be slain. She must look at a situation and say, "I see the ocean waves coming at me, and if I'm not careful the undertow will get me." As soon as she can predict that, she will be able to take command and the situation will not be a reliving of the dream.

Sandy must, in the end, live a life in which she is "Free to Be, You and Me," as the record by Marlo Thomas and Friends is titled.

After I gave a draft of this chapter to Sandy to correct, the profound effect of this simple dream began to gain momentum. The type of insight she has gained and has applied to daily living is exactly what every therapist hopes for. The remarkable part is that a dream should have provided the impetus for change.

As she read the chapter, she reflected on her earlier desire to have her parents read it. She had hoped so much that they would gain an awareness of what had happened during her growing-up years and, if at all possible, respond differently to her. However, she sadly realized that her mother would respond with only one conclusion: "Where have I as a mother gone wrong?" This would be her only response to Sandy's therapy. It would be no different if her mother read about the process, no matter how dramatically it illustrated the way Sandy is changing. Then she became aware that a sense of helplessness has always pervaded her feelings toward her mother. How could she become an effective person since her relationships as a child had been ineffective? Therefore, it is very understandable that she now felt completely at the mercy of others.

Sandy and her husband went on a vacation trip to the mountains with her parents after the preceding sessions. As she was helping her father prepare the campsite, her mother suddenly said, "Oh, remember how you used to help me put up the tent and get the camp ready? And the other kids never wanted to help. But you were always right there. We used to have a nickname for you. We called you Old Faithful because you were so trustworthy."

Sandy reported her reaction: "As soon as she said that, it hit me so hard. Oh my goodness! That is the name for my whole past. It's the meaning of my entire childhood. Old Faithful! That hit a chord in my inner being like you wouldn't believe. That is how desperately I tried to win their approval; but I never could. Nevertheless, I just kept on trying and trying and all it earned me was a nickname. I was a victim of this desperate need to please people, and it was so obvious to everyone. No wonder I am where I am today.

"Ordinarily, an episode like that would have given me an awful headache, a stiff neck, and all kinds of other physical symptoms; but all I experienced was a little lightheadedness. The insight I received was so great. I was so thrilled that I didn't have to take it out on my body."

Several days later Sandy's awareness of the meaning of the dream was put to a test. She had all the insight at her fingertips, and she could use it to cope in an entirely new way. This is exactly what one must do to make the greatest use of a dream. Dreams are meant to give a person an important message and the person must then respond.

Sandy received a telephone call from the elderly woman referred to earlier. This was her journal entry following that call.

Hi J. [That's what I call my journal.] I feel pretty good this morning. Guess who called. My 83-year-old friend. Chatted a bit. Before she hung up, she said, "I think you crossed me off your list or something." I didn't know what to say. I just can't deal with her at this stage of my life. To me, she represents my living for everyone else, not for myself at all. That is what I am running from at this time. I have to be free to be me. While we were talking, I imagined waves lapping at my feet, with the undertow hiding beneath them. In my mind I was running up the beach, and I went to sit on a big strong rock. Yeh! It didn't get me this time, and I have victory after that call.

This incident was not followed by the lightheadedness or headache Sandy was so prone to suffer from when a guilt trip was laid on her, as this woman had learned to do so effectively.

Then another journal entry.

Hi J.

My husband is such a joy sometimes. He just left for work. He said less than five words to me, and he wouldn't hug or kiss me. (Sigh) It created an empty void in my chest and stomach. A feeling related to resentment.

I told myself it wouldn't control me and drag me away. I'm bigger than his silent game. . . . His reason for acting this way is not really important at this time, since I am writing this out, and I am dealing with my emotions.

That was a fairly big wave. The undertow even had a mean face and lots of big teeth. I turned and ran up the beach and climbed up on the boardwalk. I stumbled at times, but I did get away. (Yeh!) I did it again! Two days in a row! I have a touch of lightheadedness, but it will go away.

Several days later there was another incident which in former months would have left Sandy a physical wreck. Before, she had no handles to deal with it. She was simply at its mercy, and the physical symptoms would have disabled her until she was a complete victim of her crippled body. She wrote about the incident in her journal and closed with the statement:

I've been getting more and more lightheaded. My neck and head are tightening up. I think this time it's a big wave. I can't run up the beach. The undertow is closing in.

It won't get me, even if I have to crawl on my hands and knees, one step at a time.

Wow! I reached my black rock. That's as far as I can go right now. It's safe here. I feel better.

I have no doubt that Sandy's recurring dream was symbolic of her whole struggle in life. The waves were the early warning that she was about to be confronted with a predicament she would not be able to handle. If she allowed it to happen and did not intervene in some effective way, then the undertow would take over and she would be swept away to sea. The end result was a whole series of disabling physical symptoms which merely transferred her emotional and interpersonal helplessness into physical helplessness.

An individual is more capable of dealing with physical pain than with emotional pain, so the body has a built-in mechanism to substitute a lesser symptom. The emotional situation is more dreadful because there is no end in sight. The person is caught in a helplessness spiral that has no end; ultimate death seems to be the only answer. So the body pain at least incapacitates the person to immobility.

There was no way for Sandy's psyche to get the full meaning of this message through to her, other than through a dream. All my counseling during the previous months had only had a modest effect. However, once the dream could be recognized, we both knew that we were now at the deepest part of the pain in her life. The fact that the events were so simple made them easy to recall. Now she only needs to identify, in her fantasy, any incapacitating event as waves, the moment it begins. She gauges the enormity of its control by the size of the wave. If she can respond at this point, then she must visualize herself fleeing up the beach. For herself, she has identified the exact spot where the water ends and the stretch of beach begins. There is a big black rock that is an intermediate shelter. Then, finally, the boardwalk is ultimate victory. Of course, there is the powerful undertow which has to be contended with. To get into that makes matters much, much worse.

The beauty of this dream is that Sandy could use it for a very precise understanding of her life. However, even though the fantasy is a valuable tool and helps to create imagery when any potentially destructive event is occurring, she knows that this is not the end. Sandy must obtain mastery of her life by gaining greater insight into herself and her past, and by discovering effective interpersonal skills. Once the most vicious demon of her life is slain, then she can continue to grow.

Several months later Sandy described a situation she was struggling with, which contained all the features that crippled her. A woman with a severe physical disability had struck up a relationship with her. Sandy felt an obligation to reciprocate. But she soon realized that the woman's friendliness was combined with her demand for absolute perfection in manner and behavior from all relationships. This meant that Sandy had to agree to several telephone calls and at least one visit and lunch weekly, on an exact schedule. The woman claimed that friendship must be under her own control, since much of her life was beyond her control because of her disability. Sandy was deeply moved by the woman's plight, but the penalty was a relationship entirely on the other woman's terms and very little on her own. Much as Sandy wanted to be kind, a situation like this brought out all her terror of being overwhelmed by other people. In the therapy hour she decided she must terminate the relationship entirely.

She had no sooner arrived home than the ritual telephone call came. This time she chose to answer it, which she had not done for days. Now Sandy told the woman that due to her "perfectionism," she could no longer continue the relationship and wanted to terminate the scheduled calls and visits. She was very kind, telling the woman that this was due to her own inability to deal with such exactness. The woman was confused by the request, but accepted it. Sandy hung up, feeling victorious at finally having the courage to take care of her own need, rather than always giving in to the needs of others.

The following night she had a repeat of the ocean dream. She was far out in the water with a number of people. The weather was overcast, it was dark and gray, and the waves were big. It was in every way a terrifying experience. Then Sandy realized there was no undertow. She decided to get out of the water, and she now could do so, even though the waves were high and the shore some distance away.

As soon as she woke, Sandy realized that her escape from the terror of the ocean was directly related to her escape from the overwhelming relationship the day before.

After giving this account, Sandy burst out in a loud exclamation: "Isn't it neat! How exactly my dreams show me how free I have become!"

There is no question in my mind that the full exploration of a simple dream was the breakthrough in this therapeutic process. The key to Sandy's healing was to accurately identify the personality problem portrayed in the dream, and then to deal with the problem by using the imagery of the dream. As soon as Sandy could respond, the dream changed from capture by the undertow to victory over the sea. When she is free at last to live her own life, Sandy's dreams will stop tormenting her.

A Single Dream—A New Life Begins

8

Can one dream transform a person's life? Yes, I believe this can and should take place at times. In this chapter I will illustrate how it happened to the Reverend Faith.

If a person is ready to accept the full impact of such a dream, life will be suddenly and profoundly changed. It is as if a sealed trap door of the unconscious is blown open and years of hidden mysteries come billowing out into awareness. After that comes the crucial test: Is the person able to receive and understand the message? And equally important: Is the person ready to respond to its plea? If so, then we can ask God to step in and work miracles far beyond our expectation.

For Faith, the timing was exactly right, as it always is with dreams, and she was ready to hear the whole truth. This, too, was no accident.

Let me now prepare you to understand the events of the dream. I shall address her simply as Faith. We are on a first name basis, as I am with most clients. She identifies me as Abe in her journal entries.

The real drama behind the dream began in her childhood. Faith was a psychologically abused child. Her most painful memory is the time her mother called her into the living room to meet guests, saying, "Come in here, Pud, and show us how fat you are." As an only child, she had no sibling to help her discover inner or outer resources to cope with such derogatory comments from a parent.

It was exactly this type of double message received in childhood that she later expected in all meaningful relationships. First her mother would lure her into an interaction that appeared to be loving, only to follow it with a violent rejection. At that time Faith could not understand this, other than to feel a sense of worthlessness and to distrust all relationships.

As a way of winning authentic reactions from her mother, she often cleaned the whole house and did all kinds of extras. Then when her mother came home she would call out, "Look, Mommy, what I did for you." This evoked only a moment of pleasure, and then would come the sarcastic comment, "And why the hell didn't you do . . ."

Other double messages were far more subtle. First the mother would chide Faith about her overweight: "You look like a barrel with the bands kicked off." Then she would pile Faith's plate high with food and not allow her to leave the table until it was all eaten. As a result, Faith learned to be numb to all emotions inside herself, because they were so inconsistent she had no other way to cope with them.

Faith's response to her childhood was to view all later relationships as having the potential for disaster. She vowed never to trust anyone, because as soon as she did they would "sock" her down. She said, "I sifted all my interpersonal experiences through my mother's grid." In other words, in every relationship she now expected people to eventually reject her, no matter how positive the initial encounter. As you will see, she expected the same thing to happen in therapy.

In a later entry in her journal she wrote:

I have always tended to choose relationships with rigid, controlled, emotionally withholding men. This is my own need to protect myself from the fear of genuine intimacy on any level. For me, intimacy equals dependency.

During her seminary years she met Ron, to whom she became engaged. It was the drastic destructive interaction in their relationship that brought the two of them to seek help from me.

Her yielding to this relationship with Ron was motivated primarily by her need to play it safe. Ron was a dependent and needy person who spent his energy clinging to her for support. She was very sure he would never turn on her. He was far too weak to do that.

For a period of three months I saw Faith and Ron in premarital counseling. This was a very frustrating experience for all of us. Ron exercised all his passivity, as he had always done. If I gave explicit instructions, he would obey them, but that was all. He wanted no insight into his pattern, nor did he want to change it. To make matters worse, he also assigned the complete "care, nurture, and feeding" of himself to Faith. However, he still wanted the courtship to proceed and ultimately wanted them to be married. He appeared pasted onto her, and that is where he wanted to stay, sanctified by marriage.

Obviously Faith could not endure this long, because she really wanted a vital relationship. So she took the initiative to end the courtship.

This action was very difficult for Faith. Ron evoked all the charitable needs that had motivated her into the ministry in the first place. The more she responded, the more helpless he became. When she finally took responsibility for a dead-end courtship, she evoked enormous guilt in herself. No pastor who preaches love should ever hurt anyone, but should, like a shepherd, care for her sheep. And Ron was the helpless lamb. When he realized that the counseling was about to end their relationship, he simply vanished. This left Faith feeling as if she had just thrown her own baby out on the street.

After this phase had passed, Faith wanted to continue in therapy in an effort to deal with her problem, which had preceded Ron. I accepted the change of purpose willingly. Unfortunately, very little happened. Faith was able to talk about a lot of issues, but everything was shallow. I felt she was aloof and distant. I knew she had much unresolved personal trauma, but she was not ready to take advantage of therapy for that purpose. She became exceptionally quiet, sitting back in the farthermost corner of the office and waiting for me to direct the interaction. I honestly did not know why she thought it worth her while to come.

There was one fact that made matters even more confusing. Faith could speak the language of therapy, of emotions, of interpersonal interaction. Since she conducted growth groups herself, she often used information from our sessions to help others. This always left me wondering whether that was all she expected. She was using me as a supervisor for her own practice, and maybe—just maybe—she was getting what she wanted. Whenever I expressed doubt about continuing the sessions, she vetoed it abruptly because she said she wanted help. If she wanted to be helped at all, she must take ownership of her own emotions, her feelings, whether negative or positive—fear, joy, loss, or whatever they might be. She had to permit herself to experience the vital center of her life.

I exhausted all my skill as a therapist to reach her. Largely out of my discouragement, I decided to end the therapy. Even this suggestion brought only the reaction that she wanted at least one more session.

Then I made a therapeutic error. I failed to remember that the next session was to be the final one. When she came in, I proceeded just as we always had, only to be rudely awakened when she criticized my failure to remember. Since Faith was so angry and upset, for once her true emotions erupted, and they were all directed at me. I acknowledged my error, but then realized the value of her angry outburst. It showed that she was able to come out of her shell. If this were possible, then we should make one more effort at therapy.

I must be honest in admitting my major reason for forgetting that this was Faith's final session. I had put so much effort into the sessions, with so little result, that I was no longer paying much attention to her progress. The whole thing seemed so hopeless, and I had no idea why. Faith could not tell me. She did not talk about how she felt, so I assumed that therapy mattered little to her.

All this was changed by a single dream which Faith had several nights after that session. She wrote out the dream in full in her journal and immediately afterward, proceeded to write pages and pages of new insights.

The first phase of the dream focuses on her extreme difficulty with intimacy.

May 29

Abe and I are in my parents' living room. It's a therapy session. He is supposed to be there. I am unaware of why the switch in locations from Souderton to my hometown but it was apparently scheduled that way. I expected him there.

I'm incredibly tense. Abe is asking me questions. I'm barely able to respond. Can feel the blood rushing—head pounding, palms sweating. Am trying desperately to recall the items I wanted to work on in the session—continue to draw blanks.

Suddenly Abe's whole countenance changes. He appears to take on supernatural characteristics. When he looks at me, his eyes penetrate through me and he can see my entire inside. His ears are so keen he knows every thought I have. Nothing can happen but that he already knows it. As soon as I think of my childhood he already knows it all and what it means. When the thought of the relationship with Ron erupts he instantly understands everything. Suddenly I realize that I will be totally exposed. Nothing can be hidden from him. He will know all the secrets of my heart. There is no escape.

Total panic—I want to run away, but I can't, because he already understands that. I want to scream, but he tells me to go ahead, it is understandable if I do. I am revealing all that to him also.

At last I am caught. There is no way out.

Incredible fear—meant to run away.

Blank space . . . (The terror of this moment was so great I can't remember what happened in the dream.)

Doorbell rings. We're both seated as before. I'm still struggling to talk—not succeeding. I must, but I can't.

Abe answers the door and follows an adolescent boy out the door. It's winter—snow and ice on the ground. There's a blue station wagon parked at the curb, loaded with kids and adults.

I'm furious that he got up and walked out, since there is still 20 minutes left in the session. He tells me to come along.

I squeeze into the back seat of the car, but am aware he's not there.

The car moves about 10 feet and stops. Abe sticks his head in the window and tells me to get out.

I follow him to the back porch, telling him I want the last 20 minutes of the session.

He whirls around to face me and tells me with intense anger: "I've got three things to say to you.

"You were glad when the doorbell rang, because you were looking for a way to avoid the session and dealing with yourself. You got up and left."

I try to interrupt to tell him he was the one to leave, not me. But he goes on . . .

"Three times during this session our relationship crescendoed and you put the lid on it. I'm wondering if in all close relationships you cut people off when you feel they're getting too close.

"And third . . ."

I woke up before hearing number 3, totally stunned at the accuracy, and incredulous at the dream. It took quite a few minutes for my head to stop pounding.

We later interpreted this dream together and understood it clearly.

First, it was obvious that the change of location in the dream from my office to her parents' living room indicated that a major shift in intensity was necessary. Instead of the casual aloof encounter as symbolized by my office, she needed to personally reveal herself, her feelings, and her intimate life struggles as symbolized by her parents' living-room setting. The incredible tenseness and the rushing of blood to her head showed how extremely frightened she was of such revealing in therapy. In the dream, just as in all previous office experiences, she drew a blank and could not say what she really needed to say.

The next part of the dream switches to my role as a therapist. I should know the truth about her inner being. I would know those hidden thoughts, facts, and feelings and understand their meanings, if she trusted me enough to reveal them to me.

When the whole truth of her overwhelming fear hit her, she panicked. She even drew a blank so that she could not recall what happened.

The ringing of the doorbell and my being called by others simply meant that I was to end her treatment— that I would go on to help others. The adolescent boy symbolized another client.

I believe when I told her to get into the station wagon it

symbolized my telling her to leave therapy if it could not be what it ought to be.

When the ultimate truth of her loss struck her, she pleaded for the remaining twenty minutes. In the dream, her soul was telling her she wanted another opportunity.

The statements I made to her in the dream are exactly what she felt I should tell her—that it was her fault therapy had not accomplished its task. I might have made an error, but she could not blame the failure of therapy on me. She must take responsibility for the risks she was afraid to take.

Immediately after the dream, the following insights which she recorded in her journal show a meaningful change. After the dream she knew exactly the direction she must take in order for therapy to be effective.

The awarenesses keep coming. I feel as if I could use two hours in therapy this time. I'm still living with the dream—incredible! . . . The tears and the sense of loss when he told me the next session was termination put me in crisis for three weeks. Literally hours of intense crying, never being able to exactly put my finger on what I was losing—only knowing that something very precious and valuable was going out of my life. Only now do I realize how intensely I felt termination, even to the point of going to pieces.

Really the loss is my losing the opportunity to finally get in touch with my own person. Down deep, I knew he could lead me there, but I was too afraid to let this happen.

Then, going into what was supposed to be a termination session and finding out that he hadn't even remembered making the comment, "Next week, termination." I'd grieved over that so intensely for three weeks, and he simply forgot.

Had I done it? Was it my fault? I knew Abe only terminated the "impossible" to work with, game-playing type cases. Was I game playing?

My God—the feelings of rejection, inadequacy, hurt, fear. Now how would I ever get out of this prison?

When I went back into therapy and shared my fear of the termination and the anticipated grief process, his response was: "This is the first time I have heard you say that therapy meant this much to you. I always had the impression that you could take it or leave it. I even felt it mattered no more than that to you. You talked as if I had an important place in your life, but I could never feel it."

All my life I've been frightened by the intensity of my feelings. Incredible fear around my crying—not being able to control it. Have put more energy into rejecting, controlling, denying my feelings.

Abe was in touch with that part in me from the very beginning: "The way to get you to feel better about yourself is to get you to feel good about your feelings."

Funny—I never realized until the dream how inappropriate and unentitled to my feelings I had seen myself.

After that dream I have learned that merely being in touch with what I'm feeling inside is not equal to fully giving myself permission to completely experience the feeling and accepting it as O.K.—no matter how intense, how scary, how stupid the feeling may appear to be. The key is in permitting myself to have all my feelings—not merely catalog them and then shelve them.

I remember how, as a kid, when someone called me Fatso or Stupid, I'd feel the tears start to flood my eyes and the tightening in my stomach. I'd fight like crazy to be in control. Never let them know they'd hurt me.

In seminary the unwritten motto of the women was Die, Before You Cry. I was so saturated with hearing, "Women are too emotional to be pastors. Women are irrational. They don't deal well in crisis situations. Women fall apart," etc. etc.

Then I hit the parish—the ultimate challenge in terms of completely eradicating my tears when brutally confronted. Oh, I've cried lots—bitterly, intensely, until I couldn't breathe and my eyes were glued shut—but, by God, they'd never know they'd succeeded in hurting me.

I know when I'm in pain—when I could cry—but I save it 'til later. There's not one human being alive I trust with my tears—to judge me as weak and emotional and irrational. And when I look around, the things that seem to hurt me most deeply don't seem to faze anybody else.

I need to learn to see my feelings as valuable, listen to them, allow them to guide me, and see my apparent supersensitivity as a blessing rather than a bane.

Abe's comment that Ron's attraction to me was that my strength would make up for his helplessness was only surface. The corollary—that I would be able to help him out of his helplessness to independence—stuck in my mind. I needed a guy who was so weak he would never force me to face my own feelings of inadequacy. That is Ron.

I believe, now, that's my previously inexplicable attraction to Abe as a therapist: that by relating to someone as "whole," as fully feeling and so celebrative about the intensity of his feelings, he would eventually pull me out of my dungeon.

Hence the intense grief over losing something so precious. The first healing process in my life, and I was discarding it. It's like losing part of me that I haven't yet found, but want so desperately to find and learn to love.

Yes, Abe, I fear getting too attached—I do back away. I do put the lid on relationships where I fear the pain of an anticipated ending—where I fear being seen as out of control, weak, emotional, when I come face to face with someone so whole, so comfortable with his feelings that my own discomfort and fear of my own feelings stands out in bold relief.

In a later session Faith stated succinctly what the dream had done for her.

"That dream was like an explosion of insight, all at once. It had a profound effect on the therapeutic process. I had had a problem getting in touch with and owning my feelings for so long. No matter how much we talked about it, that was not enough. Now I know exactly what you have been trying to help me with. Wow!

"What made the dream have such an effect is that I remained in the twilight zone, as you call it, for days and days. It was like a revelation during a twilight talk with God. I understood enormous amounts that I probably would never have understood without the dream."

From then on, I dealt with an emotionally transformed woman. Nothing was ever the same again in the office. She now erupted with emotions—screamed for joy at new insight, or wept with sorrow over the hurts of childhood and the tragic loss of her lover. She was now free to be herself, free to feel, free to understand, to be angry. And we both agreed that this was the miraculous work of God who had stepped into her life and touched her in a dream and called her forth to live.

Finally, in a letter granting me permission to use the journal entry, she said, "I must admit that I'd forgotten some of what you'll find in these pages. The fact that it represents the most genuine and intense feelings I've ever been brave enough to put on paper is the only thing that gives me the courage to share them with you. I'm celebrating the fact that they are the product of our therapy which I value deeply. Thanks!"

Shortly afterward, Faith had the courage to resign her church to enter a doctoral program in one of America's finest graduate seminaries.

It is from that perspective that I later asked her to respond to this material. Was the dream really a transforming experience? If so, how? Here is Faith's written response.

I have come that you might have life—life in all its fullness (John 10:10*b* TEV).

Dear Abe:

Christ's words indicate to me that we have within us the capacity to know life in a deep, meaningful, vibrant way if we experience it in relationship to our Creator and Redeemer. New life comes through relationship, not only with God, but with our fellow human beings. The grace of God revealed in Christ becomes manifest in the world through the power of human encounter.

What does all this have to do with dreams? The dream recorded in the preceding pages of this chapter, and the learnings gleaned from it, were significant for me. The dream was a turning point for my life, in that it made clear to me the extreme poverty of even my most cherished relationships. The learning was initially a painful one: Although it contained promise and a vision of greater wholeness, it also challenged me to risk on still a deeper level, a price I wasn't sure I was willing to pay, given my past history. The picture was all too clear—the choice was mine: to continue to settle for less than what I now knew to be possible because it felt secure, or to move out and test the limits.

The past year has been a rich one—full of opportunities to learn and grow through relationships. The doctoral degree toward which I am presently working is in pastoral counseling. The academic demands represent only a fragment of the entire program, for the underlying philosophy is that as a child of God, I am able to minister to others in direct proportion to my understanding and experiencing of myself.

The dream was a point of awakening. The journey toward wholeness is a lifelong process for each of us—a God-given challenge and a gift of potential. The seed of that potential has been nurtured in me by those who have loved me along the way, and it will continue to grow as I continue to nurture it in myself in relation to others. My responsibility lies in taking the message seriously—in attempting to actualize the potential God has given me. God speaks to us in many ways—through the Word as Scripture, through grace-filled relationships with one another, through dreams which reveal our deepest selves and enable us to know ourselves in ways that lead toward fulfillment—greater potential for fullness of life, which would otherwise remain hidden from our sight.

This chapter is significant in that it illustrates how a single dream, correctly understood and appropriated, can transform a person's life. The most insurmountable barrier to growth is revealed, and can then give the dreamer the choice of overcoming the obstacle or bypassing it. It is possible to make such a change, because now, possibly for the very first time, the person can see the exact barrier to growth, which has been dramatically clarified by the dream. To know what one has to deal with is half the solution. Then to do something about it is the other half. That is what happened to this client.

Now we were ready to begin therapy. Now we were ready to deal with the real emotions, the real Faith, the real problem. The wall she had spent a lifetime erecting to keep from ever being hurt again was shattered by a single dream. The person who had been hiding came out to face the world, face the hurts, face the joys. The emerging person could now make peace with her past, take responsibility for her present, and choose the future that was awaiting her.

After an experience like this, I want to shout to everyone who will listen, "Look what your dreams can do for you. Why will you not take heed? Your dreams can be the key to transforming your life. Why don't you learn this language of the soul?"

The Work Is Yours, Lord Jesus Christ

9

Sometimes God speaks very clearly through a dream. Not only was this fact true for the Patriarchs of the Old Testament, but it is also true for us today. Of course, it is absolutely necessary for us to believe this before we can hear God's voice in our dreams.

Most people do not believe or do not know that God speaks through dreams, so they miss the message. Thus a whole channel of communication is closed between God and humans. It is very sad that such a beautiful avenue of dialogue is not often used.

No, God does not suddenly arise as a glorious blazing personage in the midst of our sleep to point a finger at us and say, "I want you to go . . . now!" But he does appear with messages that are just as clear. However, we need the capability to hear the messages.

The whole question of the way God speaks to us is very nebulous to most people. Some claim to find his voice exclusively in the Scriptures. As they are meditating on a text, suddenly one particular passage hits them with a precise meaning, and they know they have been in touch with the Maker. But they may fail to be in touch with God in the mundane routine of everyday living. It is foreign to many to walk alone in the sun and yet reach out and clasp God's hand, or to stand lovingly over the crib of a sleeping child and suddenly be overwhelmed by the magnitude of God at work—these are the kinds of experiences some never have. When a crisis is brewing, few people know how to quietly call on their Maker to say, "God, this is yours to handle, not mine." How many can quietly enter a situation with the full certainty that whatever the outcome, God is still at work? The possibility that God might speak to them in a dream may elude them altogether. If they cannot hear God in daily events, how could they hear him in something as mysterious as a dream?

I would like to illustrate exactly how God spoke to me in a dream. It was his voice, beyond the slightest doubt. I knew it; I heard it; and I obeyed it. Afterward, I was filled with total peace and confidence, whereas I might have been deeply distressed and full of doubt. My purpose in sharing this is to suggest how God speaks explicitly in a dream, and to explain how to understand his voice.

I should emphasize that by the time I had this dream I had spent years listening to my dreams and had heard many messages. I was already attuned to listening and believing what I heard. I was prepared for this moment. This is important to know, since the growing, learning, awareness process does not come all at once. I believe it is like spiritual growth in other areas of life—one must work at it.

In order to understand the significance of the message I received, it is first necessary to describe the situation and the events that preceded the dream. I have made a deep commitment to seeing pastors in individual or marital therapy. I am aware that this fills one of my unmet needs, since after I graduated from seminary, I turned away from the pastorate to secular graduate education. I have as many as twenty-seven ordained ministers on my caseload; this answers a very deep question about why I felt called to seminary but did not follow through. I am often referred to as "the pastor's pastor."

To facilitate this process I have established a very close relationship with a number of regional denominational executives from whom these referrals come. A local bishop and his staff use me at times as a referral source when a pastor is in trouble emotionally. Members of the staff have become my friends. Although we are not of those denominations, my wife and I have become attracted to various congregations because we enjoy the powerful growth-oriented preaching and the beautiful people we have come to know.

As time went on, I began to hear rumblings about a long-standing and deeply distressing problem in one congregation, centering around the senior pastor. Some years ago the governing board had insisted that he be restricted to adminstrative duties, to permit the younger, more dynamic preachers to occupy the pulpit. The senior pastor was not accepting of this arrangement, so he frequently used his power position in a very disruptive manner. Attempts were made to have the older pastor removed from office. However, due to his position and his length of tenure such a move was very difficult.

Unexpectedly, I received a request from the senior pastor, who insisted on coming to my office for an appointment. He was in trouble and needed to be bailed out. He was quick to tell me that the bishop had strongly recommended the appointment.

Thus began a year of regular consultation-supervision-therapy sessions. I have deliberately hyphened the three words, since the exact purpose of his visits was always vague. At times, it was all three. He also had the unique ability to prevent it from being any of them. At first he told me he came because the bishop had told him he needed help personally. His relationship with the other pastors and the congregation was always strained. No one seemed to know how to relate to him. His domineering personality and overbearing mannerisms were offensive to many parishioners.

I was aware that he needed help. I did not question this, but I often wondered if he would accept it. I also had some doubt that I was the appropriate person to help him. At least he had agreed to see me and probably would see no one else. My highest hope was to rescue him from the disabling interpersonal relationships which were damaging both him and the church.

After a number of months, he trusted me sufficiently to unveil a frightened human being behind the facade. At this time he revealed the story of his childhood. He had grown up with several siblings in a slum neighborhood, with parents too poor to spend time or energy discovering his emotional needs. He was the only child who had received advanced education.

During this period of our time together, we enjoyed what appeared to be a beginning degree of success in therapy. He could lower his barriers and unearth much of his life story. The pieces seemed to fit together. He gained insight, and his anxiety level was greatly reduced while he was with me. He could, at times, translate that insight into better functioning on the job.

I invested a lot in this man. I wanted him to succeed. In so many ways he appeared to be the right person for that church. I wanted to help him. I felt this was God's will for both of us.

As time went on, he began to report more and more problems at the church. The trouble directly concerned him and his failure to give effective leadership, but he conveniently blamed everyone else. He could not deal with confrontation in therapy, and I could feel him withdraw.

He reported that his subordinates had met with him to say that they needed direction from him, that they cared about him, that they wanted him to continue as senior pastor. They even asked what they could do to facilitate this. Instead of hearing what they were saying, he put up his guards and justified his position. After several more attempts, they finally notified him that they had called a meeting with the bishop because they could no longer cope with the impasse. During this time he exhibited a lot of fear in the sessions, and often looked haggard. But at no time could he own any error on his part. For him, the problem was all out there. Several times he hinted at the suspicious similarity between what I was saying and what the bishop was saying.

Then one day in my office I had to deal with an angry man. He told me that I had betrayed him. In the first place he had never asked for therapy, but only wanted me as a consultant, and it was my need to make it something else. As far as he was concerned, the bishop had applied undue pressure on him to come to see me. The bishop had never clarified whether this was to be consultation or therapy. The pastor said that I was, in a subtle way, defining him as the problem, whereas jealous fellow pastors were the ones at fault. Then he accused me of collaborating with the bishop.

The reason for the accusation was the similarity between what the bishop and I were saying. Therefore, he assumed we must be sharing information. He said he now understood that the purpose of these sessions was to make him the scapegoat for a nonfunctioning congregation. I could only register my utter shock. I did not know what else to say as he left my office.

I felt very bad that night. I reviewed the entire process with my wife, who is my professional confidant. Yet I found no resolution, since I wanted to see the process to completion. Now, I could not see how this could be accomplished. The success of this person and of the church weighed heavily on me as I went to bed.

Then I had a dream which gave me clear direction. I will share the dream exactly the way I experienced it, delaying the interpretation until later. I suggest you read slowly and carefully, forming an analogy between the dream and the preceding drama.

I feel that something very important is about to happen. Then I become aware that the location of the event is some distance away, and I am urged to proceed in that direction. Soon I notice other people beginning to move ahead also. As the crowd increases, I note that all these people are from the village of my childhood. This gives me a feeling of kinship, because I want to be with them; they are my people, although I do not recognize any individual by face or name. The size of the group increases until it is a huge multitude. They greet me as they pass; they smile and accept me.

I am momentarily startled by the fact that I had left the village almost thirty years before, yet these people recognize me. Next I become aware that I have a very important part to play in what is about to happen up ahead. I feel good about that, since I know I am qualified for the task.

I sense there is to be a holy mission, and I am very blessed to be called to perform it. Then I realize that this crowd does not know what is about to happen, just as I do not. Also, they do not know it involves me in any way. They do not know what I have done with my life, three thousand miles away from their village. How could they know? This explains why they take me for granted, just as they do one another.

For a moment my eyes catch the attention of some complicated plumbing that I know was to have been completed before this day. I am startled to notice that it is finished and was done correctly. I marvel at the ingenuity and the dedication of the person who put it together. I pause long enough to be grateful for this individual who is cooperating to make this event successful. I say something to the effect that it is just great to be a part of this committed group, such as the person who did this job.

Then I stop to look left and right, and I notice that a number of other preparations have all been completed just as they should have been. There is some sense that I know who has done this work and that I had known the person would do it well.

A temporary stairway made of wood comes into focus ahead of me. This was also built by several people who helped prepare for the event. Again, I am aware of the diligence that went into making it.

Just as I begin to climb the stairs, I feel an agonizing pain in my lower back. It is extremely painful to climb the steps, but I must bear the pain and struggle upward. I sense that I would not absolutely have to do this, but I decide that the event is so important I must accept the pain. I, too, have an important role to fulfill, so I go on.

Hordes of people are climbing the same stairs. They push to get around me. No one pays any attention to me nor stops to help me. At first I am somewhat surprised by their behavior, but then I conclude that they do not know I am in pain. So why should they help? They are concerned only with where they are going, just as I am. After a long, hard, painful struggle, I reach the top of a plateau and sigh with relief.

I now notice that all the people are going off to the right and left, as if there are aisles. Then they file into the center to make up a huge audience. This is all happening some distance beyond. "Wow," I say to myself, "what a beautiful sight. What profound worship we shall experience."

Immediately in front of me, I notice my oldest brother, who has just assembled a very complicated contraption.

The purpose of this device is to siphon gasoline from one car to another. There is an air about this device that is very, very important, because it is the solution to the gasoline shortage.

My brother is waiting to demonstrate it to me, so he is eager for me to arrive. I then realize that the idea of purchasing this apparatus was mine and that I paid for the total cost, which was great. It is extremely elaborate, but I already know all about it, because I have studied its making for years. My brother had only assembled it from the enclosed instructions.

He is the only one who knows my role in procuring this device. He will soon move it in front of the audience to demonstrate how it works. There is a sense that this device is very unique, that it will greatly benefit my older brother and the entire group. That is the reason for this gathering and the air of expectancy. It is also clear that my brother will be recognized and rewarded for developing it, but I will not. The machine will greatly facilitate what he is to do with these people and will make it possible for him to fulfill his ultimate calling in this setting. The device and his knowledge of the way it works is the key. As for me, I will benefit only in the same way as the audience.

Next he switches on the device so I can see how perfectly it works. We are all amazed at its precision and at how well it will fill its role. I watch as finely tooled copper wheels turn—the cogs fit perfectly. There are clear plastic tubes at various places where I can see the gasoline flowing. He looks at me with what appears to be genuine gratitude. His expression says, "See what you helped me do. Thanks a lot."

Just then he removes the hose from the car into which it is pouring gasoline. He says, "Oh! I forgot. I need to do something else," and with no hesitation, he pours the gasoline all over my trousers. This is a very deliberate act—he moves the hose from side to side, beginning at my belt, then carefully down one leg all the way to my shoe, and then down the other leg. After this, he inserts the hose back into the car. I look at him, and he has an angry, accusatory expression, as if to say, "Look what I can do to you. How come you didn't know that, or expect that from me? You should have known that I could turn this device on you, no matter how much of you is involved in obtaining it. You idiot!"

My first reaction is bewilderment. Why would he do this to me? Why, at such an important time, just before its use will be demonstrated, when I had done so much for him so completely unselfishly? Just before the highest moment of success for both of us, he humiliates me to tears and makes fools out of himself and me. How awful!

In an attempt to understand his motive, I pick up a large assembly instruction catalog. As I examine it carefully, I realize that I know the contents very, very well. It is exactly what I had spent years and years learning. The procedures described are standard and universally accepted. I have seen every page many times, and I have used the book frequently.

I search through the text to see if there is anything said about my brother's behavior. Suddenly, I notice that there is a cautionary note which says that at any time along the way, the person operating the device may squirt me. Then I realize that I already knew this, and I am embarrassed that I was caught so totally off guard. I tell myself that I should have remembered and taken precautionary action. However, now it is too late. My brother comes out the victor and I am the fool.

After this, I pay no more attention to the device or to my brother. I become preoccupied with the hideous mess on my pants. I am utterly humiliated and in a state of shame. I wonder what these people will think. How can I explain? More important, how can this great event be redeemed?

Just then, I realize that no one else has seen what happened. The people are all in their places, up ahead, and do not notice me. Since nothing has been said about my involvement, why should anyone care? They don't know anything. The device is now my brother's possession. He doesn't need me, and he can do with it as he pleases. I am beginning to wonder now what he will do with it, now that he has turned on me. Will it, in fact, achieve its purpose? A temporary fear crosses my mind. Will he, by chance, turn the hose on the key people, or on the audience as a whole? I thought he needed me for the actual demonstration and the follow-up management.

I begin to retreat. As I do, I notice the same stairs behind me, and I can easily leave. It won't matter how messed up I am. That is good, and I quietly begin to descend the steps. Remorse, bewilderment, and irritation are my deepest feelings, but at least I can leave unnoticed.

At that moment I hear the audience singing loudly and clearly the German song, "Die Sach Ist Dein, Herr Jesu Christ." The English translation is "The Work Is Thine, O Christ Our Lord."

As I gradually awakened, I could hear the words of the song over and over. I could understand only the first line, but the music and singing continued throughout the verse. It was perfectly clear that these words also were part of the answer to the concern I took to bed with me. God had just told me that the situation was not mine to deal with, but his. "The Work is Thine, O Christ Our Lord." I did not need to bear the burden of this pastor or of the congregation. I was relieved of it and God would take over.

The congregational mess was not mine, but God's to

clean up. The pastor was in God's care, not mine. So why be distressed? It was out of my hands.

My sensation, as I awoke further, was one of perfect peace, tranquility, and comfort. Whatever I was to do, I had done. The rest I must leave to God, and I would do that, too.

I still needed to decide exactly how to turn it all over to God. I knew I must, but I did not know exactly how. What was I still obligated to do professionally? We had not finished. What did the congregation or the bishop expect of me? I decided to write out the dream, and then tell the pastor that our work together was over, that God had told me in a dream to terminate.

I had no sooner finished writing than my doorbell rang. It was the pastor. He still appeared distressed. He rather abruptly told me he was through with me and that the problem of the church would be worked out without me. I was totally dumbfounded, since I already knew our relationship was to end. I meant to read the dream to him, but then decided against that because it would seem that I was merely using it for my advantage. In his state of mind, it would only enrage him. So I chose not to share it.

After he had left abruptly, I went into deep meditation and prayer, continually marveling at a wonderful God who is at work in this world and in my life. Then I interpreted the dream, item by item.

Most prominently, I heard the hymn. It kept floating through my mind, even as I reviewed all that had preceded it.

Why do I say that was God speaking to me? Simply because I feel that God speaks directly to spiritually sensitive people through their inner experiences. There is where I want God to meet me. So that is where he speaks to me. I do not need any further proof or argument. I have heard him clearly in my own dreams and in the dreams of others, on so many occasions that I accept this as true by faith.

As I reflected about this marvelous fact, there was an internal glow of satisfaction. I would accept the message from God and obey. The whole work—the pastor's life, his calling, his growth, the future of the church, the work of the congregation, and the bishop—the whole *sach* ("work") is God's.

When I had established that, then other parts fell into place. The mass of human beings symbolized by the villagers were really my brethren in the Lord.

The purposeful movement of the group in a specific direction was really the call of the church to do its task of Christian witness in the world. The dedicated sense I experienced in the dream was exactly how I felt about all those people in real life. The one major obstacle, at this time, was the senior pastor. At one moment, there appeared to be resolution for this, too. That was why the crowd was assembling—to hear him and see him perform with a new freedom. However, this was to be done without me. I must exit and God must enter. I accepted that.

Instantaneously, I identified the image of my older brother as that of the pastor. His higher position of authority was, I felt, very similar to that of my brother during my growing-up years. The device I provided for him was my therapeutic method and skill, with which I had been familiar for a long time, and now I was turning it over to him for his benefit. I had paid for it. I had studied its operation. I was well versed on the inner workings. It was I who knew that it was the answer for him, and later for everyone else. That is exactly how I saw my role as a therapist in his life.

The person who had done such an excellent job on the plumbing was the bishop. I even vividly recall looking at it in the dream, being pleased that he had completed it so perfectly. I immediately concluded that was what I expected of such a competent person. In reality, the bishop had contributed to the attempt to resolve the mess at the church.

I easily identified the builder of the stairway and the other workers as key members of the church who also had worked long and hard for complete resolution.

The fact that my brother should, in the end, turn the hose on me came as an absolute surprise in the dream, just as the pastor's behavior had in the final session. In each case, the very device I saw as the solution to the problem suddenly was turned on me. In both cases this happened just prior to a major step in the resolution of the conflict.

In the dream, I read the instructions again. Familiar as they were, I had forgotten one fact. The possibility that it could be turned against me was right there in print. In the therapy process, that same fact is always true. In both cases, I knew it and should have been prepared for it. People who use projection as a coping gimmick will, in an acutely stressful moment, dump their projection on the therapist. This is all too familiar to all who practice the profession. Projection is the mechanism a person uses when the responsibility of the problem can no longer be borne. He or she will find a convenient person to be the scapegoat. In some cases this will be the therapist. Like the gasoline, it was poured all over me. In the end, I came out a big mess.

In the dream, the very machine that was to be used for my brother's benefit was used to mess me up. In reality, I was accused of collaborating with the bishop to make the pastor the cause of the entire problem of the church. This was so devastating because he was making me the villain while he was telling me I was making him the scapegoat. However, he was totally unaware of this behavior. These are the life and dreams—or I should say nightmares—of a therapist.

I will take the message from God one step further. Since in the dream the audience assembling for the momentous event had begun the beautiful singing, I wish to assume there is another message, even though it was not part of the outcome. Although I had to take the backstairs and quietly go away with my bruised feelings and body, God would bring the work to completion. Whatever needed to be done would be done, though I did not know how to do it. Probably my device would be used; then again, it might not. However, I was at peace. No one but God knew how hard I had tried and how much I wanted it to work out. Like Moses, I was prohibited from going all the way into the promised land. But then "The Work Is Thine, O Christ Our Lord," not mine at all.

Dreams have a way of selecting events with spontaneity and precision so as to make a message powerful and exactly on target with what the dreamer needs to hear. The intent is that the point will not be missed, that it will be impressed so deeply that its full revelation will be vivid before the eyes of the waking person.

It is significant that the right song was used, and in the German language. The impact was so powerful I could hear the melody for many days. I even experienced a sense of submission to God whenever the song returned to my memory.

The same song had made a powerful impression on me thirty-three years before when I made my first commitment to follow God all the way. It happened in a German-speaking congregation in Saskatoon, Saskatchewan. These were my people, in the sense that we had all come from Russia, some during the last century, some as recently as the previous decade. We all belonged together, in that we spoke German much better than English. We were the first generation to leave the farm and were now attempting to find our place in the biggest city of the province. The central theme of the church was to do God's will by extending his kingdom in that community. But we did not know how—how could we be witnesses when there was such a cultural and language barrier that it was almost impossible for us to even invite a neighbor to a church service? We could not escape our heritage. We were only grateful that we or our ancestors had escaped Russia alive. Now, how does a church carry out the Great Commission in an alien environment? When our church sang, we did it with zeal and enthusiasm. We could, at least, sing to God's glory. And when it came to this particular song, a song of submission which says that in the final analysis, the work is God's to do, the entire wood-frame building echoed the message.

This impressed me deeply. It was here that I made my commitment to Christ and where I was baptized to full membership in the kingdom of God and the local congregation.

All the previous meaning of the song was stored in my unconscious. When a powerful point needed to be made in the dream, a fascinating process of recall occurred. The song reappeared with the same message, even though I had not heard it for many years.

The dreaming process exercises a great degree of appropriateness in choosing precisely the right dream to accomplish its task.

I believe that only God could have devised dreams as a means of communication. I also believe that he uses dreams to speak to us.

A Sequence Multiplies the Message

10

A series of dreams can provide the impetus for profound personality change.

As I present this story I feel I am on holy ground. I know I am taking a chance in permitting Joy to reveal such extremely personal information. I trust that you, the reader, will also handle it with reverence.

I would like you to understand Joy, so that the events and emotions of her dreams will communicate the full depth of the intended message.

Joy, the oldest of three children, was born into a very poor family. She was continually criticized by her mother, and her father had no relationship with her other than to spank her for anything she did that he did not like. Joy's most vivid memory is of a belt being lashed across her legs. Her feelings about herself were that she was simply a "bad, bad, bad girl." To this day, her emotions still scream out at her, "Bad girl!"

For Joy, childhood development was one long painful process. She received a very poor sense of her own worth. At about eight years of age, she was dared by classmates to lie down and expose herself. She did so because of her desperation to gain approval. When a teacher came to her rescue, she became aware that she had committed a shameful act. The teacher reported it to the parents, who were mortified. They expressed their utter disgust with her behavior, and she was later tormented by the same children who had encouraged her. She developed a tick in her shoulder, severe enough to keep her from school for a year.

Joy was always depicted as a crybaby. En route to and from school, she remembers being pushed, hit, and knocked down by children day after day. When her father came near her, she cried for fear he would punish her, and then he would beat her for crying.

The exposure incident was so deeply embedded in Joy's soul that for the rest of her life, whenever she expressed herself or was forced to assess herself, those scenes from her childhood would come back to her. It always seemed to be the ultimate in degradation. She had a nagging sense that in the final analysis, she was a defective person anyway. It is necessary for me to emphasize this here, because it is a key to the recurring symbolism that emerges in the dreams.

Joy struggled long and hard to try to cope with all these bruises from childhood. Because of their lasting effect, she felt as though she were deformed.

On the positive side, Joy is acutely sensitive to her own emotions, and to those of everyone else. She reads body language quickly and accurately, an art she perfected to survive her childhood. This high degree of sensitivity is often the outcome of acute pain during the development years.

Joy is now married and the mother of several children. About eight years ago she experienced an in-depth spiritual transformation and soon afterward joined a community group that focuses on the recognition of spiritual gifts as part of their ministry.

However, the strange thing was that no one in the group could cope with Joy's spiritual insights. Her gift was so intensely personal and intuitive that it caused others to panic. Therefore they told her she had the spirit of Satan and was a fortune teller. They said her messages were too long and too repetitious; that they were messages of death, not life; and that surely this could not be the work of the Lord. She was told that even the motions of her body, which are central to the praise service, were seductive and revealed unconfessed sins. Again and again, she was confronted and made to confess "false spirits" and acts that she had no memory of performing. But somehow the group saw evil in her anyway. Joy, wanting to be the compliant person again in order to gain acceptance, confessed, though it humiliated her to feel like the scum of the earth.

During the five-year period, Joy continuously sought deliverance from the so-called "spirit of divination." The members of the fellowship were sure that she was possessed, and they told her it was up to her to be delivered from it. She did all she could to be rescued. When they asked if anyone wished to be delivered, she would eagerly kneel in front of the assembly, and people would place hands on her head and pray for her.

At other times she ran from one member to the next in a desperate search for some clarity on this whole matter. In return, she would receive another blast of pious confrontation that would send her to her knees, begging for deliverance from this "possession." Often when alone she moaned and groaned for relief, and even this was seen as the voice of Satan in her, and more prayer was needed. Although she was totally willing to do anything and responded to every call for healing, they still said it was her fault she had not been rescued.

At times like these, memories of that childhood scene returned, convincing her that this was the evil from which she needed to be cleansed. Since that event, she had been a tarnished person. Her desperate desire to win approval was played out in full again, only now it was defined in spiritual language. This experience opened up the wounds of her childhood; again her body was seen as the source of her humiliation and shame.

My conclusion is that Joy's special gift for intuitive insight is so great that this group became frightened of her. She could, in fact, read their hidden motives. Her sensitivity is so keen that no one could betray her. She knew their motives before they acknowledged them. I can only label that group's whole attitude as gift destruction, not gift discernment.

About three years ago, as a way to survive, Joy withdrew from people and formed a private relationship with God. The persons from whom she severed her ties were completely bewildered by this withdrawal.

During this stage Joy resorted to keeping a prayer and praise journal. It will help to include several entries here so that you the reader may understand the spiritual dynamics that carried Joy through a very lonely, abandoned phase of her life. The first entry shows Joy's yearning to be free from the imposed bondage.

November 8

I saw myself bound with ropes. A few people were around me, trying to cut the rope. As they would cut one rope, it would close back up again. Even a close girlfriend, trying hard to cut a very thick cord around my neck, said to me, "Joy, it won't come off." So I looked up to heaven and said, "Jesus, increase in me." After I said that, a light glowed inside me and got brighter. As it did, the ropes seemed lighter and grew smaller. So my friends tried to cut the rope again and this time the rope stayed open and came off all at once, like a shell, and out I stepped, dressed in a white gown.

January 20

I will set you in a very high position. I have called you. You will be a spokesman, a mouth piece, a prophetess. I have set you on high. You will minister to the nation. I have called you to be a leader in this body.

Several themes are repeated throughout the journal. Joy is in bondage and in pain. She sees Christ as her only source of rescue. After she is free, she will start a new life and be called to a useful task; she will heal others, even as she needs to be healed. Finally some day, a beautiful spring will arrive, and her life will blossom. Little did Joy know the role her dreams would play in that growth process.

Before her journey to wholeness could take place, Joy went through one more very devastating interlude. She had cut herself off from the fellowship of other people. They had only condemned her, so she could not go back for more punishment. During her private rendezvous with God, there were glorious moments when she poured out poetry and song, but emotionally, the solitude began to take its toll.

Joy began to crumble. That was when she called me for help. In her first interview, she described herself: "I am so empty. I am sick. Something in me is dying. If something doesn't happen soon, I will be paralyzed. I can hardly get out of the house, even to come here. I feel as though my whole being is moaning and screaming, pleading to be rescued. It is as though I am infested with a disease. It seems that I am dirt. I am scum. I have such a horribly bad self-image. I feel as if I am the odd ball in this world."

One day soon, Joy brought in her first dream. After that, things began to happen. She emerged as a vital, vivacious person who could not be slowed down or contained. We then entered the stage of evoking Joy's gift for dream interpretation.

The scene begins with two very bright beams of light shining into her bedroom. They are as glaring as sunlight and very prominent, since the room is otherwise totally dark. They shine through two small openings in the drapery. One beam enters at a low point and shines on the ceiling. The other enters high on the window and shines on the floor.

Joy is immediately conscious of several sensations. The first is that the behavior of the sunlight is unnatural. The sun does not shine like that. But there is also the feeling that it is supposed to be that way and therefore it is very good. Second, she feels that the sunbeams contain a scary important message which is supposed to make a big impression on her. She is trying to discover it when the scene suddenly changes.

Now the room is filled with a great commotion. She realizes that the ruckus is caused by a large crowd of people whose behavior is erratic, unpredictable, bizarre. The figure of a young man who is directly related to the event emerges prominently above the rest. He is not instigating the commotion, but only calling her attention to many facets of it. "Look over here," he says, as if to have her notice something very special at that location. Then he turns elsewhere and exclaims, "And over here."

Joy awoke very distressed about the latter half of the dream. It was so vivid she actually was surprised that her bedroom was not congested with people.

Then she began to reminisce about the dream, and she was certain that I would see validity in it. She said to herself that everything that happens to her is significant, so surely a dream must also have significance.

After a little reflection on those two beams of light, she concluded that both she and I had allowed light to shine into her soul. The one ray was shining from God to her, here on earth; the other, she decided, was from her soul upward toward God.

The second half of the dream, the commotion she experienced, was definitely related to the turmoil in her earlier life.

At one point she had a sudden awareness that there was a connection between the two parts of the dream. In the first part there were criss-cross lights shining, which she thought odd, since the sun simply does not shine that way.

I knew in the dream that I formerly assumed it could shine only from one direction, but now it was also supposed to shine from two directions and that was good.

You see, that is what makes my present therapy so different from the fellowship. They always gave me one answer. If they said it was a Word from the Lord, it was final. There could be nothing else. When they pronounced my spirit as being from Satan, I could not disagree, no matter how demolished I felt. But you do exactly the opposite. You continually ask me to consider all kinds of other possibilities. You often say, "Have you thought of this?" or, "Have you thought of that?" So your help represents the other beam of light. I am supposed to acknowledge that.

Then in the second scene, I am explicitly told that the fellowship was really a mob experience for me. All the babbling and yelling caused great turmoil in me. Then God directed me to look at the young man, who I now know was you. It is your task to call my attention to everything that has happened to me and to look more closely. I believe part of the mob scene represented the turmoil in my childhood. Other parts were my experiences in the fellowship. You are telling me to look back at all this, and to look very carefully because I have a lot to learn from it. I am supposed to understand what all this did to me, and then the awful confusion of my life will end.

I believe the whole message of God in this dream is that I am to trust you fully, that you will direct the process to complete healing. Light will keep on shining through you into my soul, until it will be whole, and God will shine on it all.

It was at this time that I expressed my absolute amazement at Joy's ability to intuitively reach back into a dream situation and tie it to her real experience. I even told her I could discern the gift of dream interpretation in her. She has had great sensitivity all her life. As a child and in later crises, this caused her much pain, but now it is being sanctified for a new calling—interpreting dreams and intuitively tuning in on the lives of others. Her diligent Bible study and her continuous trust in God make it easy for her to see the hand of God at work in each incident. She has a simply marvelous combination of attributes to make spiritual dream work productive. I had no idea of the consequences that would result from my affirmation of her.

In the next session, she brought in another dream, with her interpretation written out. The analysis is very brief since she was still fearful of taking too big a risk on her own. She wrote out all her dreams in full, and very explicitly, for the purpose of therapy, but I shall include only the essential portions.

As I walked into the bathroom, a man followed. He sat down in the room. I was uncomfortable, with a man there, to perform the normal function of a bathroom. However, it turned out to be no problem, and he understood my distress and brought comfort, even spraying the room without my asking. I had been worried that other people might walk in while I was there, but because of his comfort I stopped worrying.

Then some people did come in. I went over to the bathtub and drew water, while he watched me from the end of the bathtub. Someone started to get in the bathtub, but I stopped them when I saw heavy steam coming from the water. I laughed and said to them that I had forgotten to add cold water. (That's why all the steam.) I proceeded to add cold water under his watchful eye.

My interpretation: I saw I had to tell Dr. Schmitt what is

dirty and smelly. He would not label it that way and that would comfort me. And by his words, he would make what was once smelly, sweet. P.T.L.! Whoopee.

With only the slightest encouragement, Joy could go back to a dream situation and come up with more and more meaning. The fact that this dream scene was in a bathroom denotes that whatever is happening is very, very private and that that area of her life is extremely personal.

The fact that a man came into the bathroom startled me at first, but it felt so good that he understood me. I could simply trust, and there was rest for my soul. I knew God gave me this dream to tell me that I must now trust the therapy process, and you as a person, no matter what material we have to deal with. I am prone to call things unclean, but you will clean them.

The last part of the dream says to me that someday others will come to me for cleansing, as I've been cleansed by you. I will know how to temper my cleansing of them with cold water, so that I will not burn them with scalding hot water, as I was burned by other people with their harsh words. You have tempered my cleansing with affirming words, thus it has become a healing process or cleansing. Theirs were words of condemnation, thus it was a destructive process, not cleansing. One process building up, one process tearing down.

This was not the last of Joy's dreams. From then on she brought one to every session. The later dreams were much more detailed. Her interpretations were longer and more insightful. In my assessment, she got to the heart of the dreams very quickly.

The next dream was very explicit. It is sufficient to say that one of the scenes occurs on the bed, where she touches a naked girl beside her.

I saw what appeared to be a newspaper picture of people. Then, as if there were a telephoto lens, there was a closeup of a young woman in the back row. I started to get agitated at the closeup and wanted it to stop there, but it went closer and closer and showed her eyes. I cried out, "No! No! No!" Somehow, there appeared to be danger in her eyes. . . .

My interpretation after delving beneath what it looked like: I think the danger in the eyes represented a danger in seeing myself or my past. The eyes are a mirror of the soul, and I didn't want to see so deeply. I was afraid of having the past so close to me. I didn't want to see the inside of me because I considered my inside so bad that it should not be seen.

Her nakedness represented the uncovering of a private or delicate area of my past. The closeness with her represented becoming intimate with my past, or myself, which in the beginning I didn't want to do. And now, because of psychotherapy, I am starting to become intimate both with myself and with my past, and it's good.

Before I go any further with this dream, I need to clarify one very important issue. The symbolism in Joy's dreams often tends to involve intimate areas of her body, since both the hurt of her childhood and the preoccupation of the fellowship were related to the body. It must be understood that the same body sensations were replayed as Joy found healing through dreams. God was telling Joy she should find healing in this crucial area as well as in other areas of her life. How could a dream deliver messages that carry such intensely intimate meanings and such deeply distressing hurts, other than to portray them through the most private part of her body?

When Joy awoke, she pleaded with God to erase the dream from her memory. She especially did not want to reveal it to me. Her greatest dread was that if it were to be published, someone would see the contact with another female as a hidden lesbian urge. However, she quickly asked herself, "What was I feeling in the dream?" She concluded that the other person on the bed was not another woman, but herself. She was touching her own body and the sensation was "good. It is beautiful. I am starving to make peace with my body and God is leading me to do it. I may have to have outrageous dreams, but thank you, Lord, for your divine revelation. You are indeed leading me to wholeness—of my body, my mind, my emotions, and my soul."

Then she wrote out the dream, knowing she could turn it over to me.

Again, it was difficult for Joy to locate me in the dream. I kept asking her, but she simply blocked. Then I explained that I was the lens, forcing her to focus on the person in the back row—herself, always hiding in the background so as not to be noticed. I moved the lens closer and closer until she met herself eyeball to eyeball. She then realized that "the eyes are the windows of her soul."

Why did Joy struggle so hard against recognizing my role in the dream? Much as she wanted help, she was terrified of me, as she had always been of men. And all her past terror was surfacing again in the therapy hour.

The belt slapped across her legs in early childhood was felt again and again. She also reexperienced all the destructive authority that men had exercised over her. Now she must run the risk of revealing these hidden parts of her inner self to a man. But the value of this was that by doing so, the healing was much greater. I was, indeed, the lens that was held in front of her, and everything must be looked at. But she also knew that I would bring out everything so gently and delicately that, no matter how frightening or ugly the dream, I would lovingly accept it all and then hand it back to her "sweetened," so she could accept it and possess it. She trusted my healing ministry and knew that I am called by God, just as she is and that we are both accountable to him.

Now I was ready to take the next step in evoking Joy's gift of dream interpretation.

The fourth dream is a very elaborate drama. Joy finds herself bathing in a public place, with a mirror reflecting her every move. She feels intense pleasure, since she has discovered that her body is good because it is her own.

> It was mine. It belonged to me, and it was all right. I found myself nodding my head and saying, "It's good," quite pleased with the whole thing. I continued to wash and was quite unconcerned that the shower curtain was open, and so was the door to the outside. People were watching. When some people moved closer, I suddenly seemed to notice that I had a shower curtain and I felt the need to close it.

Immediately after recording this dream, Joy made a quick note of the interpretation. Now she could also react to her own emotions about the process.

> I am disturbed that Dr. Schmitt will have to know about this dream, too. I feel that people will think the last two dreams are pornographic and will be offended. Lord, why are you giving me these dreams, and then wanting others to hear about them? Good things come disguised. I'm not healed enough not to mind what people would think if they knew it was I who had dreams like that.
>
> There is good progression in these dreams. I'm encouraged. This dream caused me to really think: Of what am I being cleansed? What is the most intimate part of me?

After two days of reflection, Joy came up with a full interpretation.

> Dr. Schmitt's office is a place of cleansing for me. Others have been cleansed before me, and now it was my turn to be cleansed of the burdens of condemnation placed upon me by others, and also by myself—to be cleansed of my hatred of

myself; to be cleansed of my distrust of people because of having been hurt by so many; to be cleansed of my need for approval, so that I might walk in wholeness.

His words are like the mirror, a reflection back to me of myself; that I must see the most intimate part of myself. Because of the questions he asks to make me think, I am learning about that most deep and hidden part of myself, which I've not been acquainted with before because of my need for approval and of trying to be only what others wanted me to be. I'm beginning to see the real me. I sense that there is goodness there—where I thought none existed. While continuing the cleansing process with him, I will become more open with people, more willing to reveal the real me to them.

However, because the process is not yet finished, I will sometimes feel threatened when people come too close, and I'll feel the need to close myself off from them. That is when I want to close the shower curtain.

I do not think this dream needs any further interpretation. Joy did a profound job, without any aid from me. She has discovered her intuitive gift of experiencing life at great depth. When she uses this gift with her own dreams, the true meaning is unlocked and she comprehends it perfectly.

There is no need to be afraid of this gift. The individuals in the fellowship were fearful of her ability, so they dumped all their terror on her body. Now that she can own her acute sensitivity and exercise it as a gift from God, she is blossoming like a rose at the height of springtime.

Even though Joy's dreams were sexually suggestive, I thought it necessary to include them because I hope others can be freed to own their dreams, no matter what their symbolism. It is only that dreams attempt, or may I even say that God attempts, to make a very emphatic point. The degree to which one is alerted, or distressed, or embarrassed in a dream—to that degree the message is in need of being heard. It may require imagery that is uncommon, but the imagery doesn't matter—pass it off and get in touch with the emotional message. Symbolism only makes the message easier to understand and easier to obey. It was Joy's request that I emphasize this so that no one will pay too much attention to the symbols in their dreams. "I want people to get in touch with their unusual dreams and then be free to understand the interpretation. It is my prayer that this will happen for many people, and that is the only reason I release my dreams for others to read. I want God to be glorified by them."

In our therapy session, Joy and I celebrated the marvelous working of God in our lives. Joy, who had seldom remembered a dream, was now experiencing the most vivid dreams, with such explicit messages. She had discovered the gift of understanding. This had meaning for me in that I had been able to recognize and evoke the gift in her. The whole experience had led to a transformation in her life and her family.

At one time she had stood hunched over, a direct consequence of her poor self-image. "My whole body revealed that the burden I was to myself was too much. I am beginning to stand straighter. When I'm finished, I want to stand tall and face the world with confidence. I am a child of God. I am cleansed. I have nothing to hide. I am not a 'bad girl.' I will face the world as a person with special gifts to be used to the glory of God."

Joy and I were ready to end the series of dreams at this point, but it was not to be. Shortly after the last session, Joy had another dream which, in her words, "rounded everything out." God knew better than either of us that this was necessary.

"I really feel you need to hear it. I had quite a time with this one. I had said, 'Lord, no more dreams, unless you really want to give me one.' I guess it was not nice of me to say, 'no more.' So here I had one that puts all of my life into focus, as well as all the other dreams, in spite of my begging not to have more and my concern about it. I stayed up until past one o'clock last night, writing it out for you."

There were some people sitting on a stage in front of a television camera. An announcer, with a microphone in his hand, stood facing the stage and was talking about illnesses. He announced to the unseen audience, "There are many people with this particular illness. Someone has offered to show us how this illness affected her."

A little girl about eight or nine years old, who had been hidden behind people, came forward. She came to the edge of the stage, facing the announcer and the unseen audience. The announcer instructed the little girl to expose herself.

I was horrified as I watched all this take place. "Oh, no," I exclaimed. "They shouldn't ask her to do that! She'll be damaged if she does that in front of all those people!" I felt so bad for the little girl, having to go through the humiliation of public exposure, and I was worried about how this experience would affect her.

Hesitantly, she did as she was told. As she sat in front of us on the edge of the stage, with a shy, half-afraid look on her face, we could see the damage. For plainly on her young body were the scars and marks of the illness. She sat there, facing the audience, with a willingness to stay long enough to allow us to absorb the full impact of the damage.

As soon as Joy finished reading the dream, she said, "I know you know what that represented. I knew what it meant when I woke up. However, putting it down in writing was more difficult."

Soon afterward, she wrote out her interpretation. She was very certain she knew exactly what it all meant. The interpretation, as she wrote it, is included in totality.

May 9

Dr. Schmitt is the announcer and I am the little girl. He is writing a book on dreams and he has asked if I would allow my dreams and interpretations to be included in his book. I am hesitant. These dreams and interpretations are very graphic and reveal my innermost thoughts. I am shown as a little girl in this dream because that's where the illness started. The illness is the lack of self-worth, shared by many. It is apparently necessary for others to see the damage and extent of the illness. Perhaps that they might have hope for healing, as they follow the progression of the dreams and see the healing that's taking place in me. There is a television camera there, so that the message might be seen by more than just the few in the studio audience, as Dr. Schmitt's book will reach more than the few people I might come in contact with and tell my story to.

As I watch this take place, and as he is writing about my dreams, I am afraid of being hurt by the exposure of that which has been private to me.

But I sit here determined to allow these dreams, which are not pretty but distasteful to me, to be put in his book if there will be benefit to those reading them. I have gained peace from the interpretations, which show me that that which seems gross can have a deeper beauty if it is brought forth. As, hopefully, the traumatic things in my life will produce beauty in me.

I wonder if the readers will be turned off by the graphic part of the dreams, or will they look beyond the ugliness and see the beauty of the interpretations?

For several days Joy reflected on the dream. Flashes of insight hit her. Then she decided to rewrite her interpretation.

May 12

At this stage of my life, I have come forward from the hiddenness of my past and, at the bidding of Dr. Schmitt (the announcer), have exposed the private part of my childhood to him. He has known my illness and the damage that was done to me while I was young.

I was frightened, at first, at the idea of public exposure of that which was private to me.

But now I am willing for the damage to be seen by the unseen audience of Dr. Schmitt's book, as he uses his pen as a microphone to communicate the words of his mind. The damage could not have been seen in the quick glimpse of only one dream, so there are several dreams to graphically show the damage that this illness—this lack of self-worth—did to me. But hope and joy is seen in the progression of the dreams and the healing that is coming. I stand on the edge of this stage of my life, looking forward to the next, with the sure knowledge that that which had been traumatic in my life has now been used for good.

We have now returned to the scene at the beginning of the chapter. A little girl exposed herself to a group of her peers and was frightened for many years. I do not mean that this effect was the result of the one incident. The personality scars occurred in all her relationships, especially in the home and with the children in the neighborhood and school. It was only the most repulsive act that became enlarged in her confused mind. Then in the final dream, another little girl sits on stage exposing herself. Only now, it is in a ceremony of healing—of healing through a dream.

It is hard to imagine that a dream could use such exact symbolism to pinpoint Joy's problem precisely, and then so explicitly show her how the healing must take place.

There she sits on stage. In the dream she is in the studio audience, but she knows even then that she is also the little girl on the stage. As the little girl, she exposes the fearfully scarred parts of herself so that real healing can follow. This also indicates that she trusts me, since I direct the scene as she observes herself facing the most painful part of her past.

She knows that the audience in the studio is made up of her friends, to whom she may tell her story.

The television audience is composed of the many persons who will read this book. Joy knows that all this will be viewed by a great audience. However, now she is not ashamed because, as in the dream, our intent is to glorify God and to enable others to be healed as she was healed.

The message in Joy's dreams is profound. It must be understood that she was in therapy when the dreams were analyzed and also that she accepted complete responsibility for the message.

To review a sequence of dreams such as this leaves me breathless. It is beyond my imagination how precisely a dream could portray Joy's deepest struggle, or that of any other person who cares to learn the language of the soul.

Closure

11

In this final chapter I want to answer a series of questions. Some have been alluded to in previous chapters, so I will summarize those. In other cases I shall highlight issues I think need to be raised.

How far can a person really trust a dream?

My answer is very simple: all the way, provided it is correctly understood; or not at all, if it is misunderstood. A dream can bring a ray of insight into one's life at exactly the right moment to direct one's path. For this to happen, one must be keenly tuned in to the inner meaning of the dream, and then connect that to the inner working of one's current life. At the same time, faulty use of dreams can be dangerous. This is especially true when another person is involved in the dream and the dreamer lays the burden of the message upon that other person. An even greater misuse would be to invoke God's authority to do this.

A prominent novelist spent months working on a book. As she was nearing the end, she suddenly realized that she could not bring it to a proper conclusion. She had become so carried away with the body of the story that she had lost her way. In desperation one night, she pleaded for God to speak to her and help her conclude the book. True to form, she had a dream in which the ending of the novel was symbolically played out in full. She immediately completed the story and praised God for his miraculous intervention.

I am not really surprised. That is exactly what dreams can do. I do not mean to minimize the power of God to speak through dreams. I believe the author's prayer was sincere and that it was answered. Yes! I would even call it miraculous. Dreams, by their very nature, take what eludes a person and reveal it. I believe she had a vague awareness of how she meant the novel to end, but in the course of writing, lost it, or simply could not put the pieces together in her conscious mind. In the dream, the unconscious took over—without the fears and apprehensions, without the distractions of daily living—and rearranged the material in the way she had meant it to be. To unscramble all that so easily is miraculous, and she should praise God for it.

As I was sharing my whole theory of dreams with a close friend, he had a clear memory of a similar event. While he was in graduate school, he had agonized deeply over the subject of his final project. Suddenly, it all flashed before his eyes in a dream. He followed the instructions explicitly and was able to complete his degree.

What is the primary purpose of a dream?

I believe the major intent of a dream is to bring into focus a current issue that has become blurred in the clutter of living. I have repeated that theme throughout this book. A dream highlights what is really important but which, for some reason, the individual has not recognized or has not accepted. The dream, in some familiar drama, will confront the person with the full impact of that meaning.

A young couple spent the evening talking about the man's switch of majors in graduate school. He kept explaining to his wife that the matter had to be kept totally secret, since it could jeopardize his present degree and his admittance to the next program. They made explicit plans about keeping it from their peer group in the same university and church fellowship. She was not aware how deeply this distressed her until a dream followed that discussion.

The dream opened at a congregational meeting where her husband was the subject for the occasion. Gossip had spread that he was gay and the church had an open meeting to decide what to do about him. She violently protested that it was all a lie. She was extremely upset, but her husband remained perfectly calm. He was willing to permit them to believe what they wished, while she was ready to protest violently and demanded that he stand up for his rights.

She awoke still very disturbed. However, she quickly made the connection between the dream and the discussion the night before and concluded that she was far more concerned than she had known, about living with the secret information. She also realized that she really did trust her husband totally. No matter what happened, he had a calm, rational way of dealing with it. If the information were disclosed, she would fall apart, but he would not.

After relating this dream and her understanding of the message, she remarked, "That message was so loud and clear I could not have missed it, but did I have to be hit over the head with it before I recognized it?"

I responded, "A dream has a very specific message, and the dream will contain whatever is necessary for you to understand that message."

Does a dream always call for a response?

The very nature of a dream calls for a response. A dream is intended to give one the opportunity to do something that is needed about some phase of life to which one has failed to give attention. My repeated dreams compelled me to write. A deep inner part of me was telling me to pick up my pen. I did not have to obey, but many dreams contained the same message. As soon as I responded, there were no more such dreams.

I believe dreams recur because we have failed to yield to a message. Often the simple recognition of the request is sufficient response. At least then the meaning is brought into the open and an individual has the opportunity to consciously debate the pros and cons of what needs to be done. Some recurring dreams end after they are recognized, even if we do not follow through. However, there can be a great reward for responding, as the following episode illusrates.

A middle-aged single woman obeyed a dream and made a very specific response.

Her mother was dying of cancer. For the last several years she had often been called to her mother at crucial life-threatening moments. To prepare for these emergencies, she enrolled in a CPR (Cardiac Pulmonary Resuscitation) course. This dream followed.

She again received the alarm in her dream, and dashed to her mother's residence. The mother was gagging. The daughter immediately applied mouth to mouth resuscitation, but to no avail. Something was lodged in the mother's throat. She then resorted to the other techniques she had learned in the CPR course. They also were unsuccessful and the mother died in her arms. A dreaded sense of failure overcame her. She had put all that effort into preparing herself for a moment like this, and yet she had failed the test with her own mother.

When she had told me the dream, I asked her to reflect on its therapeutic value. I urged her to respond to the message and gain insight in therapy. She is sensitive, intuitive, and brilliant, and immediately allowed herself to reexperience the dream from the depths of her soul.

"First of all, it tells me I am very keenly aware that my mother is dying. I guess I am on the alert at all times that the next telephone call may be the final cry for help. The dream tells me I must bring this to full consciousness and ask myself what else I must do to be more ready to face that too.

"Then when I saw her on the floor, and she was dead, I was startled by that sight in the dream. This helps me to mentally visualize that whenever or however I find her, I must be ready for it. I now allow myself to think of all the possibilities.

"The really good part about this dream is that she died only in the dream and not in real life. So now I do have the opportunity to prepare myself before it actually happens.

"The dream highlights something very, very real to me. I am a guilt-ridden person. My mother has always used guilt to control me. When I was unsuccessful in reviving her, I felt all the guilt of a lifetime surging through my body. I could almost hear her say, 'See, I died. It's your fault.'

"After I woke, I had a conversation with myself about the degree to which that guilt controls my behavior toward her, and to what degree I am doing the sensible, expected thing. I concluded that it would be very easy for me to look at that dream and double my efforts to do more and more for her before it is too late.

"I decided I will no longer let guilt rule my life. I am doing all I can possibly do. If I do any more, I will jeopardize my profession as well as my health. I concluded that the dream stopped me short, to reevaluate my role in this dying process, and for once I gave myself a passing grade. This is a big step forward for me, and it will help me live with myself after she is gone.

"The deepest therapeutic value for me is that it forced me to preview my mother's death so explicitly, as if it had already happened. I have often thought about it, but the dream made me live through it as if it were true. Now I am ready to face it when it does happen."

Should one respond to dreams? I have only one answer: Why not? It can lead to such meaningful growth-producing results.

Does the symbolism have any special importance?

I believe the symbolism is important only in that, at the moment of the dream, it is the best the unconscious can use to make the desired point. There is a similarity between the depth to which one feels symbols in the dream drama and the issue in real life that needs to be recognized. The intent of the dream is to make an emotional impact with whatever is necessary to do that. The dream appears to be totally undiscriminating in its selection of theme. Some dreams are shocking, but that only calls a person to sit up and listen more abruptly. I believe that dreams often occur in a childhood setting simply because one experienced life so intensely at that stage. Therefore, it is perfect material to be reused in a dream. Sex and violence also cause deep arousal of emotions, so their inclusion in dreams serves the same function. I believe the choice of symbolism serves no purpose other than to make the dream emotionally analogous to real life.

Now this book is almost finished, and naturally I should expect a dream to reward me for this accomplishment. Last night I had a dream that did exactly that.

I find myself in Banff National Park. My whole family is in the car and we are peacefully driving north toward the ice fields. It is all very familiar, since I sense that we have been here before. The towering mountains are as gorgeous as I expected them to be. We are impressed, but I sense that this is a repeated trip. "This is all very nice, but why are we here again? What special occasion made this possible? I can't grasp this." I try to understand, but I can't. I struggle with the issue even as I participate with the other family members in the very pleasurable occasion.

We suddenly realize that the scenery is so beautiful that it must be photographed. One bend in the road has brought us the perfect view. The sun is shining brightly and there are billowing clouds in the background. Everybody gets out of the car and I photograph them and the scenery. I am especially aware that my son-in-law and future son-in-law are present. My wife is there, as well as our four children, and everything feels right. Suddenly a deer steps out into a clearing and stands there as if to deliberately add to the beauty of the scene.

I look at my camera and examine it carefully. I am overcome with that moment. Why is it that I have the right camera, at the right spot, with the entire family present to be photographed?

I awoke in a state of perfect peace, with a feeling of euphoria. I repeated to myself, "The exact right timing, the right spot, with the right peple." Then I realized that this was the perfect day to finish my book. That is exactly what the dream meant. This day was to be set aside for writing; there were no clients to see or schedule to keep, and I was especially well rested. My mind was clear and sharp and I was ready to push my pen. I paused long enough to thank God for his marvelous plan for the creation of humankind, including the magnificent way he included dreams in that plan.

But lest I become too overwhelmed by this dream, let me call your attention to how perfectly the dream analogy fitted the real-life event. The symbolism served its purpose exactly.

The scenery at Banff called my attention to the fact that this moment was very profound. When I saw it nine years ago, I was overwhelmed by its beauty, so a replay is perfect, if that was the impression that dream sought to convey. Everything else converged to give the message: "You are at the right spot, right now."

The symbolism told me that today is the right day to finish this book, and that is what I am going to do. I may take it one step further and say that the dream and my experience today are God's will for me. I equate the trip to Banff National Park with the trip I took in writing this book, although that part was not clear in the dream. What was clear is that at that moment I was where I should be; so I wake to where I should be today.

God has spoken to me through dreams, and I have obeyed. My hope for you is that you will ask him to speak to you in every possible way, including the way of dreams, and that you, too, will experience the joy of obeying his call.